FISH

54 Seafood Feasts

Cree LeFavour
Photographs by Antonis Achilleos

CHRONICLE BOOKS
SAN FRANCISCO

Designed by
— SARA SCHNEIDER —

Food styling by
— GEORGE DOLESE —
&
— ELIZABET NEDERLANDEN —

10 9 8 7 6 5 4 3 2

— CHRONICLE BOOKS LLC —
680 SECOND STREET
SAN FRANCISCO, CALIFORNIA 94107
WWW.CHRONICLEBOOKS.COM

FOR DWIGHT GARNER

AND FISH

CONTENTS

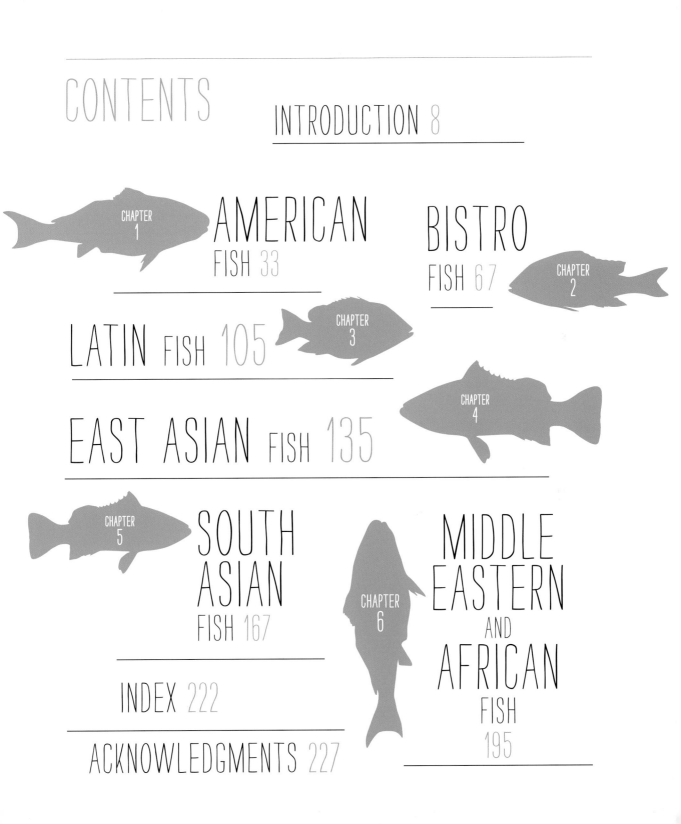

INTRODUCTION

— AS HUNGRY AS —
THE SEA

When I was a kid growing up on a ranch on the Salmon River, in central Idaho, the appearance of white circles on the river-bed in spring meant the salmon were running. The fish were preparing to spawn after their epic upriver swim, using their powerful tails to build nests in the river-bed, where they'd scatter their eggs. These nests, called redds, made a dappled pattern on the river bottom. The female laid her eggs, the male on standby to fertilize. Then the exhausted pair, their mission complete, would swim off to die, their bodies washing up on the rocky shoals where my black dog, Whitey, to her delight, would discover their fragrant remains.

Was it the many seasons of watching these beautiful fish complete their swim that made me so vulnerable to the seductive taste of Jean and Pierre Troisgros's salmon with sorrel sauce when I lifted that first forkful to my mouth at their famous res-taurant in Roanne, France, in 1978? I was thirteen. I recall that medallion of fish, translucent at its rare center, the sauce an impossible achievement: silky, with a hint of sourness and mild notes of grass, like spring butter from cows that have

been let out to pasture. That salmon was like nothing I'd tasted before. (Which is saying something, since I'd done well for myself as an eater, up until then.)

I still crave fish like that—fresh, gently cooked, and served with a fragrant sauce. I obsess over simple recipes like grilled tuna with mustard aïoli and Alaskan salmon with béarnaise. But I also adore fish done up in unruly ways—shrimp curry, spiced crab cakes, clam pie. There's a great many recipes of both kinds in *Fish*. As in my previous book, *Poulet*, the recipes here are in sets, defined by my sense of how we put meals together. I believe great ingredi-ents, simple methods, and intuitive (and sometimes counterintuitive) combinations can transform mundane meals into inspired eating any night of the week.

You'll find here sets of recipes that will make a whole dinner or a leisurely Sunday lunch. You'll also find five chapters defined by the flavors of key culinary regions around the globe: American, Bistro, Latin, East Asian, South Asian, Middle Eastern, and African. Given the rich history of immigration and the mingling of ingre-dients, techniques, and traditions in our global, hyperconnected lives, there isn't a chapter in *Fish* that's not "American." Made in America or not, the food we eat—whether it's in Singapore, Prague, or Austin—is informed by a continually fluctuating set of cultural traditions.

One of my favorite lines from a cookbook appears in Nigel Slater's terrific *Real Cooking* (1997). He explains that you can use any kind of noodles you like—"Chinese egg, Japanese ramen or Italian ribbon pasta"—in his recipe for a loosely Asian style of noodle soup. "Just use whatever is in the cupboard. Unless, of course, you are a purist. In which case you have bought the wrong book." Seconding that, I will say that if you are seeking the purest expression of dan dan noodles, as only Chinese chefs in Zigong, in southwestern Sichuan, would make them, or fattoush as it has been composed by one very ancient line of Lebanese grandmothers for six generations, you've probably "bought the wrong book."

— FISH IS FOR YOU —

A lot of people get nervous around fish. There's that indecision at the fish counter, the moral worries about sustainability, and the twinge of anxiety about cooking what you've bought (or even better, caught) correctly.

I've done three things that few if any other fish books quite do. First, I only include fish that you can eat responsibly. If I call for fish in a recipe, whether it's Arctic char or Pacific halibut, that fish is abundant in the wild and fished responsibly or farmed using methods that reputable sources agree are healthful and sustainable. Second, I've selected fish that even reluctant fish eaters will fall for because they're simply delicious. Period. *Fish* is my answer to anyone who, like me, loves *great* fish but doesn't love any and all fish. If I put a recipe in the book, I consider it dinner-party worthy—beautiful to look at and uncommonly

flavorful. Finally, I've taken these fish and put them together with a range of fresh herbs, spices, vegetables, grains, and fruits to make complete meals. Each of my recipes is easy enough for a beginner but intriguing enough, I hope, for a seasoned cook. Follow just a few of my recipes and trust me, you'll want to buy, cook, and eat fish more often. As I'm reminded every time I cook it, when fish is good, it's spectacular.

I'm a picky fish eater. I think more people are like me than not. We just want fish that's fresh and flavorful—I don't think that's too much to ask. *Fish* plays to the qualities I most love about eating seafood. Its light, clean flavor evokes a perfect day on the ocean, yet the richest fish is as decadent as the most delicate sweetbread, the smokiest chicken thigh, or the juiciest rare steak.

Fish is a great call for last-minute dinners because it almost never takes more than fifteen minutes to cook. I bring to these recipes a balance of respect and kitchen knowledge grounded in practice and science. A few of my recipes might seem daunting to anyone who hasn't cooked much fish—or cooked much of anything at all. But stick with me. If you have fresh seafood and access to decent produce and a few spices, grains, and condiments, you can be serving almost any recipe in my book within an hour.

— SUSTAINABLE SEAFOOD —

As Dan Barber, the co-owner and chef of Blue Hill at Stone Barns and Blue Hill restaurant, said, "For the past fifty years we've been fishing the seas like we clear-cut forests." This can't go on, if only because "there's almost nothing left." Gone are the days when shopping for fish required little more than sauntering up to the fish counter, chatting up the fishmonger, and blithely assessing the icy display—red-eyed snapper, briny oysters, snowy Chilean sea bass, muscular whole branzino, pumpkin-orange salmon steaks. All you needed to know was what looked freshest and best. Picking out your fish has gotten much, much more complicated.

There's no getting around it: these days you really need to know *where* your fish came from because this, more than anything else, is likely to determine if it's been conscientiously farmed or fished. As a rule, if your fish comes from the United States it has fallen under some of the most rigorous regulations in the world. (The European Union also vigorously enforces fishing and aquaculture regulations.) The careful monitoring of fishing practices (how the fish was caught) paired with rigorous enforcement of catch limits is a good thing for you, for the long-term viability of the fish you've chosen, and for the fishermen who caught it. It pays to do the right thing. The good news is, it's possible to eat well and sustainably. Let's go fishing.

BUYING SUSTAINABLE SEAFOOD

Here's my first of many confessions: I once found fishmongers to be pretty intimidating. They stare over the counter at their customers, just waiting to hear you say something stupid. At a supermarket, you can grab a shrink-wrapped chicken from the cooler, but you have to actually announce your fish order to a guy in white standing behind a tall barrier. It's a bit like announcing your prescriptions out loud to a pharmacist. Similar white coat,

similar load of judgment. What kind of fish do I want? Precisely how much of it? How do I want it prepared—gutted, scaled, boned, cut thick, cut thin? If you dare to ask when it came in, it's as if you've asked the fishmonger whether he still beats his dog.

Fishmongers are almost always men, and in my experience they're almost always jaded. Don't be intimidated. Fish is fish. Learn to know what to look for, how to ask for it, and what *not* to buy. When you tentatively ask, "Isn't that Chilean sea bass endangered?" and you get the reply (as I have), "Well, this one's dead already," you may find your feet propelling you toward the prepackaged chicken thighs, or the kale, for that matter. Stand your ground and order a pound of the Arctic char. You, like everyone else, are just trying to put a truly fabulous fish dinner on the table. I promise to make it easier.

KNOWING WHERE IT CAME FROM

The seafood listed in the tables that follow are uncomplicated choices because you don't need to know a lot about *how* the fish were caught. All you need to know is *where* your fish came from—whether it's a massive aquaculture operation in the Indian province of Gujarat or a little boat out of Ketchikan, Alaska. As a general rule, wild fish from U.S. waters are carefully managed, with regulations on catch limits, quotas, and fishing methods enforced. Fish farms from the United States and E.U. countries are generally well-managed operations that are regulated in a way that makes them sustainable. I recommend that American readers go to the online Monterey Bay Aquarium Seafood Watch for guidance on which fish to eat. British readers can consult the Marine Conservation Society's FishOnline guides for further advice. Both have mobile apps that make choosing sustainable fish—right at the fish counter—almost effortless.

Here's what you need to remember: Don't buy fish or shrimp that are farmed in Asia, including big fish- and shrimp-producing countries like China, Vietnam, Thailand, and Malaysia. When you buy wild fish, look for fish from the United States, Norway, or the European Union, where catch limits, quotas, and environmentally beneficial fishing methods are strictly enforced. Keep in mind, this list isn't exhaustive—there are plenty of other fish out there that are excellent choices. These fish are simply the most popular and therefore the most likely species of fish you'll see laid out on ice when you're shopping. For obvious reasons, I've eliminated fish from this list that may contain high levels of mercury or PCBs. I don't want to risk eating these fish and I doubt you do either.

— FARMED VERSUS — WILD-CAUGHT

You'll see lots of farmed fish on the two lists I've provided. In some cases, there isn't much of a difference between wild and farmed—think mussels, clams, and oysters, which are generally farmed in the open ocean. In other cases, the origin of the farmed fish matters because the environmental regulations outside of the United States and the European Union, as a general rule, do not provide enough protection for the environment, for workers, wild fish populations, or consumers. That means that along the production chain, a range of errors can occur that make these imported farmed fish an unacceptable choice

according to, among others, the Environmental Defense Fund, the Environmental Protection Agency, and the respected scientists at the Monterey Bay Aquarium Seafood Watch program.

For wild-caught fish, once you've determined how endangered the population of a particular fish really is in a specific geographic area, you can move on to the next question: how was it caught? There are two reasons to care how the fish was caught. One, fishing methods like bottom trawling and set gillnetting can cause extensive damage to the ocean floor or result in high levels of bycatch, including other, sometimes endangered, species of fish, seabirds, turtles, porpoises, and dolphins. You get the idea. The United States and the European Union generally do a pretty good job of overseeing these issues and enforcing the rules that are on the books. That doesn't mean the system is perfect. Far from it.

A SPECIAL NOTE ON FARMED SALMON

Virtually all of the salmon you see labeled "Atlantic salmon" is farm-raised. Unfortunately, this popular, hardworking fish that fills menus, freezer cases, and display cases from California to Maine is not, in the broadest sense, a healthy or environmentally sound choice when it comes to choosing fish for dinner. Here's why: Farmed salmon can contaminate wild populations with parasites; the genetic integrity of the wild population may be undermined by escaping genetically engineered fish; large-scale farms may pollute seawater; and, most important, since it is a carnivorous fish that requires marine protein for growth, just feeding all those salmon depletes the oceans of sardines and other forage fish. In short, it takes more protein to feed the salmon than is produced in edible salmon. Why? Salmon just aren't all that efficient in turning all those little fish, krill, and fish oil (and sometimes chicken!) we feed them into protein. Good as it might look and sound when you're staring at a fresh, carrot-colored hunk of it on clean ice, farm-raised salmon is not a great choice.

— WHY BOTHER? —
THERE'S SOMEONE RIGHT BEHIND YOU IN LINE WHO WILL BUY THAT GLISTENING HUNK OF CHILEAN SEA BASS—EVEN IF YOU DON'T

It's true that reliance on a consumer-based movement to save endangered fish is probably less effective than I wish it were. Too many people remain blissfully—or willfully—ignorant. Because not enough fish buyers are educated, the people who do make the principled decision not to buy eel, tile fish, and Chilean sea bass are doing some good, but not enough. Will there be someone right behind you in line who will purchase the fish you decline to buy? Probably. Whether he is blissfully ignorant or ethically impaired doesn't really matter. We need to do more to save a wide range of declining species *globally*, but at least you can feel you're doing your small part by not reinforcing the demand for fish that need to be left alone.

What's needed are global legislation and international treaties that limit the harvest of all kinds of fish in waters from the China seas to the Antarctic Ocean to the Outer Banks. Despite the reality that many fish at your fish market (and in

restaurants) are biologically extinct or so overfished that they lack the genetic diversity and population density to survive as a species, we still can't seem to agree that it's time to stop eating these fish. A worldwide ban on whaling was put in place through the Convention on International Trade in Endangered Species (CITES). Despite a few outliers (Norway and Japan, which continue to take whales for "research purposes"), the ban has brought back a wide range of whale species to healthy population levels. How about putting bluefin tuna, Chilean sea bass, and sharks on that same list?

If everyone lived by the ocean and knew a fisherman or two, year after year, generation after generation, you would know what you're buying and how it was it caught. You would also be pretty sure those fishermen would manage the fish population and not damage the ecosystem the fish—their livelihoods—depend upon. They would, in short, have a strong incentive to manage their own fish stocks so that they would have a large enough population for growing or maintaining their supply of fish as well as enough genetic diversity to insure those fish are healthy. Well, I don't know a fisherman and my guess is that neither do you.

Individual Fishing Quotas (IFQs) work on this principle, and they're considered by many experts as more successful than limited seasons in reducing waste and helping fishermen control and effectively manage the fish they catch and bring to market. That's because fishermen are given a set limit on a particular species or a total allowable catch (TAC). While a set season only fuels competition for limited resources, driving fishermen to catch anything and everything that swims before someone else does, or before the season is over, IFQs, and the similar Catch Share system, slow or eliminate the competition. When implemented over the long term and perceived as a permanent investment that may be held in perpetuity, bought, sold, and traded, IFQs strengthen the incentive for fishermen to manage their resources from a biodynamic perspective.

— WHAT'S THE — SOLUTION?

There are a few companies that are beginning to use microchips to label fish species while at the same time linking them to the individual fisherman and his or her boat. This is almost as good as knowing your fisherman. The technology of microchip implantation may be the answer to buying sustainable fish in the future because it

stays with the fish as it travels from where it was caught (boat and owner) to a wholesaler to a retailer and on to you.

Here's what I recommend: Think of certain species of fish the way you think of blue whales. They're not food. Period. Nobody should eat them—they're practically gone already.

BLUEFIN TUNA

EELS

SHARKS

STURGEON AND THEIR CAVIAR PRODUCTS
(UNITED STATES AND IMPORTED WILD)

PADDLEFISH AND THEIR CAVIAR PRODUCTS
(UNITED STATES AND IMPORTED WILD)

MONKFISH

ORANGE ROUGHY

TILE FISH

CHILEAN SEA BASS

KING CRAB (IMPORTED)

SKATE

Fish is one of the most frequently mislabeled proteins you'll find at the supermarket (restaurants do it all the time, too). There isn't a single third-party verified labeling system like USDA Certified Organic, or Humane Certified. One label you can look for is the Marine Stewardship Council, or MSC, label. It's a fairly reliable indicator of sustainable fishing practices, although there is some disagreement about their certification process. The MSC puts its stamp of approval on fish that are not in danger of being overfished, and on fish that are caught using environmentally sustainable methods with minimal bycatch—whether it be marine, bird, or mammal. Like most things in life, it's not perfect, but when you do see the label, you can feel comfortable that some people have tried to do their homework.

The distinction between a line-caught swordfish from Florida and one from Thailand caught with a trawler's drag net may seem academic. It's not. If you want to do your part to sustain fish populations and healthy ocean habitats worldwide, you need to ask where your fish came from and how it was caught. That's easy for me to say, right? Many fishmongers and supermarket fish counter staff don't know or won't tell you where the fish they're selling comes from, how it was caught, or if it's endangered. What's the solution? Press them for information—reputable fish markets *and* supermarkets label the origin of the fish they sell and how it was caught.

GO FISH: FISH YOU CAN EAT IN GOOD CONSCIENCE

ALASKAN SALMON
Wild. Alaska and British Columbia

Look for: chinook, coho, chum, keta, king, pink, red, silver, sockeye

ANCHOVY
Wild. U.S. Pacific and Atlantic, South American, and European waters

ARCTIC CHAR
Farmed. United States, Iceland, and Canada

Other market name: alpine char

ATLANTIC COD
Wild. Iceland, northeast Arctic, and Barents Sea (Norway and Russia)

Other market names: whitefish, scrod, gray cod, true cod, Alaska cod. ("Scrod" sometimes refers to juvenile cod, although it is also used as a common name for haddock.)

ATLANTIC HADDOCK OR SCROD
Wild, hook and line. Canadian Atlantic, Barents Sea (Norway and Russia)

Other market names: Canadian haddock and schrod. ("Schrod" may also refer to juvenile Pacific or Atlantic cod.)

BARRAMUNDI
Farmed. United States or Australian (from fully recirculating systems only)

Other market names: Asian seabass, barra, giant perch, Palmer perch, silver barramundi

BIG-EYED SCAD
Wild. Hawaii

Other market names: opelu, round scad, akule, halalu

BLACK ROCKFISH
Wild. U.S. Pacific

Other market names: black bass, black rock cod, black snapper, sea bass

BLACK SEA BASS
Wild. U.S. mid-Atlantic

Other market names: Atlantic sea bass, black perch, rock bass

CATFISH
Farmed. United States and European Union

Other market name: channel catfish

COBIA
Farmed. United States and European Union

Other market names: black kingfish, black salmon, ling, lemonfish

HAKE—RED AND SILVER
Wild. U.S. Atlantic

Other market names: ling hake, squirrel hake, whiting

HALIBUT—PACIFIC, CALIFORNIA, GREENLAND
Wild. Pacific Ocean, North Atlantic

Other market names: Alaskan halibut, Monterey halibut, southern halibut, Greenland turbot

HYBRID STRIPED BASS
Farmed. United States and European Union

MAHI MAHI
Wild. U.S. Atlantic

Other market names: dorado, dolphinfish

PACIFIC COD
Wild. U.S. Pacific

Other market names: gray cod, grayfish

PACIFIC SARDINES
Wild. U.S. Pacific

Other market name: pilchard

RAINBOW TROUT
Farmed. United States and European Union

Other market name: golden trout

SABLEFISH
Wild. Alaskan and Canadian Pacific

Other market names: black cod, butterfish

SNAPPER—GRAY, SILK, LANE, AND MUTTON
Wild. United States Gulf of Mexico and
Atlantic

TILAPIA
Farmed. United States, European Union, and
South America

TUNA—ALBACORE, BIGEYE, SKIPJACK, AND
YELLOWFIN
Wild. U.S. Atlantic or Pacific

Other market names: bonito, ahi

Warning: Mercury can be a danger in
larger tuna. Smaller fish caught using
troll and pole-and-line fishing methods
are lower in mercury.

GO SEAFOOD: OTHER SHELLFISH AND CRUSTACEANS YOU CAN EAT IN GOOD CONSCIENCE

CLAMS—SOFT-SHELL AND HARD-SHELL
Wild or farmed. United States and
European Union

Other market names: quahogs, manila clams,
razor clams, steamer clams, littleneck
clams, cherrystone clams, long neck clams,
black clams, chowder clams

COCKLES
Farmed. New Zealand

MUSSELS
Farmed. United States and European Union

Other market names: blue mussels, black
mussels, green mussels

OYSTERS
Wild or farmed. United States and
European Union

Other market names: Oysters carry the
name of the waters they are grown in.
There are hundreds of geographically
determined names for oysters, some more
famous than others.

SCALLOPS—BAY AND SEA
Farmed or wild. U.S. Atlantic and Pacific
and Mexico

Other market names: Catarina scallops,
great scallops, Hotate, lion paw scallops,
Chilean scallops, fan scallops, Peruvian
calico scallops, diver scallops

CRAB—DUNGENESS, BLUE, KONA, AND STONE
Wild. U.S. Pacific and Alaska, U.S. and E.U.
Atlantic, Australia

Other market names: gulf stone crab,
Florida stone crab, spanner crab, frog
crab, Alaskan king crab, red king crab,
hard-shell crab, soft-shell crab, com-
mercial crab, market crab, San Francisco
crab, Atlantic Dungeness crab

LOBSTER AND SPINY LOBSTER
Wild. U.S. Atlantic and Mexican Pacific

Other market names: Maine lobster, American lobster, Caribbean spiny lobster,
red lobster, langosta Mexicana, green
spiny lobster, warmwater lobster

SQUID—LONGFIN AND SHORTFIN
Wild. U.S. Atlantic and European Union

Other market names: calamari, international squid, Humboldt squid, giant squid,
calamar gigante, jibia gigante, common
squid, boned squid, summer squid, opales-
cent squid

SHRIMP—FRESHWATER PRAWNS, PACIFIC
WHITE SHRIMP, ROCK SHRIMP, PINK SHRIMP
(WEST COAST ONLY), AND SPOT PRAWNS
Wild or farmed. United States and
European Union

Other market names: spot shrimp, prawn,
West Coast white shrimp, Pacific white
shrimp, white shrimp, brown shrimp, giant
river prawn, Malaysian prawn (avoid
farmed there, however!)

— BUYING FISH —
FRESH, FROZEN, AND NOT-VERY-FRESH

Depending on where you shop, much of the fish you buy has probably dipped below freezing at some point on its journey to your shopping basket. Unless you live by the ocean and shop from a truly great fish store, my guess is that your fish has not only gone below 32°F/0°C, it was likely frozen at sea (sometimes labeled FAS) to a molecule-arresting -18°F/-28°C. This is probably a good thing. Just mind what kind of fish you're buying that's marked FAS and how you defrost it. Defrost frozen fish gently—don't run the fillets under warm water. Just place them in the refrigerator for a few hours or, if you're really in a rush, submerge them, well sealed, in cold water.

Fresh fish is unquestionably preferable in taste and texture to frozen. Its pristine quality comes through in its sweet, bright, ocean-brined flavor and in its refined texture. Still, once-frozen fish is easily better than fish that's gone a little off on its journey to you. It's unwise to adhere to hard rules about frozen fish versus fresh, unless you can see the ocean from your house. Shop for fish daily, staying flexible about what kind you buy and making your decision based on what looks and smells freshest.

What does really fresh fish look and smell like? It's actually not all that difficult to recognize fresh fish once you really get in there and apply your senses. You can also poke the fish, but I can usually *see* and *smell* how fresh a fish is without poking it to see if it's mushy (old) or springy and resilient (fresh).

GETTING YOUR NOSE RIGHT UP ON IT— SMELLING FISH AT THE MARKET BEFORE YOU BUY IT

How to smell the fish before you buy it? That's easy. Just ask the fishmonger, as I do. He takes the fish out of the case, places it on a piece of butcher paper, and extends it over the counter toward me so I can get my nose right up next to it. I exhale and take a big pull in through my nostrils with my nose as close to the fish as is (barely) polite. I do this every single time I shop at the grocery store fish counter, but I do it only rarely when I shop at the superexpensive fish market, where the fish is invariably pristine. (It's also so expensive it makes my toes curl every time I see the price pop up in digital green numbers on the scale's tiny screen.)

Fresh fish smells clean, a little like the ocean or a salty wind coming off a cold harbor. It really shouldn't *smell* much—of anything. Fresh fish definitely does *not* smell of ammonia (think bleach), nor should it smell decidedly "fishy," like the potent smell that saturates the air when you open a can of Jack mackerel to feed the cat. If fish smells predominantly fishy or of ammonia, it's probably old or has been mishandled on its way to you. Don't buy stinky fish. Ask to smell something else or move on and have fish another night.

HAVE A GOOD LOOK AT THAT FISH— GLISTENING, MOIST, AND TAUT

Imagine two pieces of cod side by side. One has been sitting around in the fish case for days at around 35°F/2°C. The other has just been carved from a whole cod that was

caught within the past twenty-four hours. The older fish is dry, with a granular, dull surface that absorbs the light. It sits lower on the ice, almost as if it's been flattened. The fresh cod is remarkably different in appearance. The surface has an unmistakable glisten and a quality of moist dewiness, which fits with its defining plump erectness. Think of this comparison when you're looking in the case at the various fish on ice. Look at how they sit up—or don't—and at how they reflect light—or don't. You'll find, I think, that some of the fish practically sparkle while others are collapsing into themselves, the mushy dullness of their aged protein unavoidably apparent. I don't think I need to tell you which fish to buy.

When it comes to whole fish, you can't see the flesh beneath the skin as you can with filleted fish, but there are other reliable clues to freshness. Look the fish in the eye. Is the eye clear black and prominent or has it clouded over and begun to sink into the skull of the fish? Look at the skin. It should be shiny and wet looking, not dull and flat. The almost metallic sheen of fresh fish skin fades as a fish ages. Finally, the gills of a really fresh fish are delicate and blood red, not brown, dull, and matted together. The longer the fish has been dead, the more dried out and lifeless the gills become. Just as you ask to smell the fish, ask to see the gills.

LOOK, SMELL, AND ASK

Terrible as it might seem, just because a fish counter is selling *some* fish that's past its prime doesn't mean everything in the case is bad. I know. You'd think you shouldn't shop at a place where the staff chooses to sell not-so-fresh fish. Well, welcome to the reality of shopping at a supermarket where they may or may not care or know better or have the authority to throw out a marginal product.

While waiting in line, I often watch people glibly order apparently old fish and march away with it in that neat white package, which feels like a gift. (Thus far I've managed to restrain my urge to run after them and beg them to return the fish they've selected and buy something else.) I guess people buy bad fish because they simply don't know better. They've never even thought about what really fresh fish looks like—and maybe they've never eaten it or if they did, they thought it was just a great recipe. Others buy fish past its prime because they decided before they arrived at the fish counter that they want haddock. When the haddock in the case is limp, dull, and stinky, they buy it anyway. Never mind that right next to it are freshly cut, glistening cod fillets that would have been the perfect substitute, no matter what the recipe.

If you shop at a less-than-stellar store, be flexible about what you buy. Make your decision once you see what's irresistibly fresh. Even before I get to the smelling stage, I identify a couple of the freshest looking fish and ask when they came in. Only then do I ask if I can take a whiff. (Just because it came in "today" doesn't mean it's fresh.)

Every recipe in *Fish* gives you alternative fish to use for the recipe. There isn't a recipe in the book that won't work with another fish. Often you can even substitute shrimp for fish—it'll be different, but still tasty.

— ICE AND THE SCIENCE —
OF FISHY FISH

Placing fish on ice isn't just a pretty way to put it on display at the store—fish keeps best at close to freezing. The unsaturated fatty acids in fish, those same ones that make fish so good for you and so delicious, are highly perishable. In addition, the amino acids, proteins, and other organic compounds that make fish so delicious begin to break down the moment the fish dies. The biggest culprit that causes that distinctively fishy smell in saltwater fish is trimethylamine oxide, or TMAO, an organic compound that naturally occurring bacteria and enzymes in and on the fish begin to convert into stinky TMA or trimethylamine. As Harold McGee, the gifted food-science writer, points out in his book *On Food and Cooking* (1984), the cold water most fish spend their lives in requires fish to have enzymes and bacteria that work well in the cold. "The enzymes and bacteria of warm-blooded meat animals" such as chickens, pigs, and cattle "normally work at 100°F/38°C and are slowed to a crawl in a refrigerator at 40°F/4°C. But the same refrigerator feels perfectly balmy to deep-water fish enzymes and spoilage bacteria." That means these little buggers can really go to town. In short, you want to keep your fish as close to freezing as possible to hold the complex processes of decomposition in check. Left at the relatively warm temperature in the interior of your refrigerator, your fish undergoes drastic changes for the worse—fast. The results are not just fishy smells but stale, flat fish with no sweetness and none of the lovely ocean brine that makes the experience of eating fresh fish such a delight. Optimal fish storage in the refrigerator is done by putting the fish in a sealed plastic bag and submerging it in a slushy ice bath.

If you find your fish smelling more potent than you'd like, consider rinsing it under cold water (you should do this anyway) and briefly refreshing it in a 5 percent salt bath. Acid, in the form of vinegar or lemon juice, will also help. It interacts on the molecular level with the stinky TMA in ways that are beneficial—at least to your nose.

When you buy clams, mussels, or oysters they should always be nestled in ice. Look for unbroken, glossy, tightly closed shells. Some shells may gape open, but should close when you tap on them. Discard any shells that are open and unresponsive before cooking. Likewise, throw out any that don't open during cooking—they were dead when they went in the pot.

Always ask for an ice pack or bag of ice when you buy your seafood, and keep the seafood in contact with the ice on the way home, especially in hot weather.

— FOOD SAFETY —
AND SEAFOOD

The truth is, eating seafood is a somewhat risky proposition. We take the risk because the flavors and textures are worth it—whether it's the slurp of a raw oyster or the beautifully clean flavor of raw tuna. Even if you aren't eating raw seafood, most fish is never cooked to a "food safe" temperature of 160°F/71°C, at which point food-borne bacteria and other microbes are

killed. Seafood may also carry viruses, parasites, worms, or toxic algae. Wow! What's the solution? Source your seafood with care and store it carefully. If you're pregnant, ill, or have a compromised immune system, I would not recommend eating raw or barely cooked seafood of any kind—it's just too risky.

— SERVING WHOLE FISH —

Whole fish have a more intense taste and they're dramatic to serve. Once the fun of the display is over, "carving" that beauty, head to tail, can be a challenge. Reconcile yourself to the fact it isn't always going to be neat. My advice is to step away from the table and, using a spatula and a fork together, lift the top layer of fish away from the vertebrae. You can do this by inserting your knife into the fish at the backbone, feeling for where the bone begins. Get under the flesh on the top of the fish, gently lifting it away from the rib bones and transferring it to a plate in pieces that are as intact as possible. After you've lifted the flesh away, you should be able to grab the head and lift the remaining bones running from the head to the tail— all in one piece. If this doesn't work, don't panic. Just remove the head and whatever comes with it, and then find and remove the vertebrae, the tail, and any remaining bones. The bottom half of the fish, the part left on the platter, should be simple to serve now that most of the bones are gone. The good news after all this fuss? Fish cooked whole is incredibly flavorful and well worth the trouble all those bones cause.

COOKING METHODS FOR FISH

Give your fish, whether whole or filleted, a good rinse under cold water before you cook it. This removes oxidized fats and other stinky organic compounds from the surface. Also, run the water in the cavity of a whole, gutted fish. In general, it's a good idea to sprinkle your fish with a pinch of salt before cooking. For more even cooking, cut a few slits in the thickest part of the fish fillet or along the body of a whole fish at its thickest points.

BAKING
Baking fish is simple and mess free. You can keep your oven temperature moderate and cook the fish gently. I recommend placing the fish in a piece of foil, with the edges crimped up to catch the juices that are released as the fish cooks. When trapped near the fish, they won't evaporate as quickly as they do on the hot surface of a wide-open baking sheet. It also makes for easy cleanup.

BRAISING
This is a terrific way to cook a piece of fish, especially if you've already got a fragrant pot full of spices, stock, and vegetables cooking. Place the fish—whole or filleted—in the liquid in a large pot and put it in the oven. Before you know it, the fish is cooked in that fragrant juice. I have a few recipes that call for wok braising, which is just cooking the fish in liquid in a wok. I guess you might technically call this wok poaching—but that sounds more like a recreational activity involving guns and dogs than a cooking method.

BROILING

For thicker fillets and whole fish, broiling is a high-temperature method that I like. Because there is no temperature standard for "high" or "low" on most broilers, there will be some guesswork involved in estimating your cooking time. If you love crispy skin and no mess on the stove top, broiling might be your method. Remember to go easy. Fish will overcook in a flash under a really hot broiler.

DEEP-FRYING

This is the big dog of messy, greasy cooking. It's entirely worth the cleanup for a big meal like fish and chips because the one you make at home is likely to be the crispiest, most tasty fried fish you've ever eaten.

GRILLING

Because most fish flesh is so delicate when cooked, it's difficult to grill many kinds of fish. You'll find you have better luck with whole fish and with muscular predator fish, such as tuna. As with any grilling, the heat of your fire matters—for gas grills most fish you'll be grilling are best cooked at a high temperature. For charcoal and wood fires, build a good fire and let it burn down to hot, white-ash embers. Clean and oil the grates better than you normally do. When you put the fish on the grill, don't move it around. Just flip it once and off it goes.

PANFRYING

Panfrying is much like sautéing, but with a lot more fat. The extra fat protects the fish from sticking, while delivering a high-temperature cooking treatment, since that oil is hot—350 to 375°F/180 to 190°C. You can crisp the skin without the mess of a true deep-frying submersion.

POACHING

This classic method is one of the easiest ways to cook fish. Because it treats fish very gently, the results can be splendid—tender, flaky, moist fish with no dried-out exterior portions. The intensity of the broth, of course, makes a difference to the flavor. A concentrated fish or vegetable stock will add flavor; with plain water you may lose a little flavor. For anyone with poor ventilation, poaching minimizes the fishy smells that can waft from the kitchen into the rest of the house.

SAUTÉING

Cooking fish in a frying pan with a slick of fat—either butter or oil—is a simple, effective method for cooking a range of fish. I particularly like to sauté thinner fillets. Because they cook so quickly, you don't run the risk, as you would in the oven or under the broiler, of overcooking. You can also keep the temperature moderate in a sauté pan by keeping the heat beneath the pan low. You won't get any of the nice browning that adds so much flavor, but you don't always need it when it comes to fish.

KNOWING WHEN IT'S DONE

James Beard advocated the 10 minutes per 1 in/2.5 cm rule. I've never been a fan of this or per-weight rules when it comes to cooking chicken, steak, or fish. (Don't even get me started on these pointless rules when it comes to roasting the Thanksgiving turkey.) No matter *how* you cook your fish, I advise checking it often, whatever the recipe's estimated cooking time might be. Every oven, grill, broiler, and stove top is different. Some fish are warmer than others when they begin cooking. Certain fish are denser or fattier than others, depending on

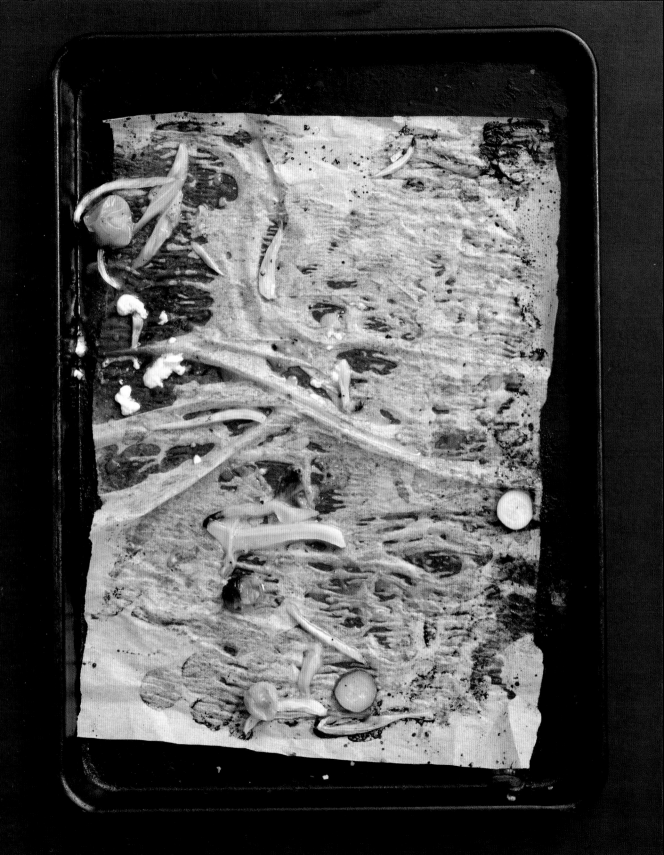

age and life cycle. Time estimates should be used as loose guides. Check your fish before you think it could possibly be done, and then keep on checking it every few minutes. Think of all that poking and prodding as an integral part of the cooking process, because it is.

The muscles that make up all fish flesh, whether red (like tuna) or white (like cod), are arranged in fine, thin layers with very little connective tissue between them. As a result, fish flesh is much more delicate than beef, chicken, or pork. The absence of connective tissue means that fish doesn't get tough, no matter what you do to it. Unfortunately, that same lack of connective tissue means most fish are difficult to handle once cooked. According to Harold McGee, fish myosin and the other fiber proteins that make up fish flesh are quite sensitive to heat. The optimal temperature for cooked fish and shellfish is 130 to 140°F/54 to 60°C. For salmon and meaty fish you may want to eat rare, such as tuna, the fish is done at a lower temperature, closer to 120 to 125°F/49 to 52°C. I love instant-read digital thermometers. Get one. It'll save you all kinds of trouble and mistakes, no matter what you're cooking.

Sadly, even if fish doesn't get tough when it's overcooked, it's a big mistake to take it way over that optimal temperature. Worse, it takes little or no effort to overcook fish. The result? Dry, mushy, flavorless flesh. Cooking your fish until it's *almost* done and finishing it in a low oven of about 175°F/80°C is one way to avoid this. Remember: fish cooks in a flash!

— A NOTE ABOUT — FISH BONES

Most fishmongers will debone fish fillets for you. Just to be sure, run your fingertips over the fish, feeling for bones. Needlenose pliers are the best tool for the job, but tweezers will work, too. Take your time. Freedom from bones in your fish is such a pleasure!

FISH STOCK

MAKES 3 QUARTS/2.8 L

If you can make chicken stock, you can make fish stock; just decide you're going to do it. When you taste this rich, fragrant liquid, you won't regret it. Most fish shops will happily give you a big package of fish heads and carcasses. For the lightest, most versatile stock, ask for non-oily fish.

2 LB/910 G FISH HEADS AND CARCASSES

4 RIBS CELERY WITH LEAVES

2 CARROTS, PEELED

2 SPRIGS THYME

1 SMALL BUNCH PARSLEY

1 LEEK, SPLIT AND RINSED

1 CUP/240 ML DRY WHITE WINE
(DON'T USE OAKY CHARDONNAY)

Place the fish parts in a large stock pot, pushing them down to condense them. Cover with cold water and then add the celery, carrots, thyme, parsley, leek, and white wine. Set over high heat to bring the liquid to a boil, skimming away the foam (and scum!) that rises to the surface. Once the liquid reaches a boil, reduce the heat to produce a quiet simmer. Cook for 30 to 40 minutes and drain through a fine-mesh colander (use a regular colander if necessary). Transfer to storage containers and freeze or refrigerate any stock you aren't using right away.

— OTHER INGREDIENTS —

PRODUCE

The ingredients you get from farm stands, farmers' markets, and your own backyard will yield fresher, more flavorful results than the produce the chain grocery store has to offer. I realize not everyone has a choice about where to shop—both because farmers' markets tend to be expensive and because not everyone has access to one or to a farm stand or garden plot. Do what you can to buy the best ingredients you can afford, and your palate will certainly note the difference.

KEY INGREDIENTS: OLIVE OIL, BUTTER, SALT

Some ingredients matter so much to the quality of your food that it's simply not worth being cheap or lazy. Among the pantry items that will elevate your cooking from mediocre to memorable are the following. Buy the good stuff, store it carefully, and watch your food get better than you thought possible.

OLIVE OIL

This may be the number one ingredient that I would recommend you take seriously. Really flavorful, fresh olive oil usually costs at least twenty dollars per liter. You'll want to go beyond "extra-virgin." Look for estate-bottled oil with a date on it—kind of like wine. You are not likely to find this kind of olive oil at your grocery store. In fact, a great deal of the oil you will find in most grocery stores is old, mislabeled, and not anywhere near extra-virgin, even if the label makes that claim. Sometimes it's not even olive oil! This is a poorly regulated part of the import market.

BUTTER

If you're like me, you think of butter as its own food group. While cooking your way through the American, Bistro, and South Asian chapters, you'll be going through a fair amount of this flavorful, gorgeous fat. I've intentionally gone easy on the salt in my recipes because I know everyone has a different tolerance. That means that you can use either salted or unsalted butter in my recipes—it'll make a difference in the amount of salt you add, but it won't alter the recipe. Use what you like, but just be sure it smells clean—no off "refrigerator" taste or cheesy smell. I love Kate's butter from Maine, which is widely available on the East Coast. Look for cultured butter, which has a richer, more complex flavor.

SALT

You'll see that I call for finishing most recipes with a pinch of flaky or coarse salt. I like my salt to be discernible as a little hit or spark of salt—with just some salt, but not all of it, fully absorbed into the food. When I call for flaky salt, I mean Maldon, the English salt with large, flat flakes. By coarse salt I mean a slightly larger grain of salt than the inexpensive kosher salt that I call for in the recipes. My favorite is Redmond Real Salt. It's a light pink color with dark mineral flecks throughout. I like the flavor and the size of the grain—not too big, not too fine. You'll find Real Salt at health food stores and Maldon at specialty food stores.

— ON TOASTING: —
SPICES, NUTS, COCONUT, SEEDS, AND GRAINS

What's all the fuss about toasting everything from farro to cumin seeds to coconut? Is it really necessary to toast spices, or is this just fussy food writer stuff? I can assure you, it's important. Here's why: Spices contain oils—which is also why they go bad relatively quickly. These oils, when heated, undergo chemical changes that release the fragrance of those oils. In addition, toasting produces that famous Maillard reaction, resulting in new, rich, and intense flavors. When we heat anything to the point of browning—whether it's farro, coffee beans, cumin, or coconut—it tastes different, and it tastes better. Between the Maillard toasty notes and the release of those good oils, toasting will up the quality of some of your most crucial cooking ingredients.

My favorite method for toasting spices is to place a cast-iron pan over a medium burner until it's hot. I then add the spices and stand there, giving the pan a toss now and again. As soon as I smell them, I know I'm close. Then, I watch for them to get a little darker. Remove your spices when they've begun to color—they'll keep darkening, even after you transfer them to a cool ramekin. For coconut and large quantities of nuts, I prefer to use the oven. I find 200°F/95°C is about right. Spread out your nuts or coconut on a baking sheet and roast until you can smell them and see that they are turning a lightly toasted

brown color. Out they come, ready to use and at the peak of flavor. When using nuts for salads and coconut as a condiment, I recommend a light dash of kosher salt to bring out the flavor. I can't think of a single nut that doesn't benefit from salt.

— HEAT AND CHILES —

There are a lot of chiles in my recipes. If you like spicy food, this will please you—if not, or if you're cooking for kids, not so much. Feel free to omit the chiles or to scale them back as you wish. Removing the seeds and membranes is one way of scaling back the heat. If I call for a habanero, one of the fieriest commonly available varieties, feel free to substitute a serrano or a jalapeño in its place. Dried chiles deliver a terrific range of flavors. I keep a few different kinds in my pantry, including Dundicut, arbol, cascabel, and Tien Tsin, as well as the unidentifiable variety someone at my community garden grew and in the end did not want—a tiny red cone-shaped chile with a thrilling, fruity fire. If you have dried chiles, use them. If they are going into a liquid and will cook there for more than 15 minutes, there's no need to soak them ahead. I buy exotic dried chiles from Penzeys Spices (www.penzeys.com). If you garden, you can grow your own. Plenty of nurseries specialize in chiles—some carry 500 varieties of chiles. Crazy! Chili pastes also deliver impressive, nuanced heat. I'm obsessed with Lao Luo Zi brand's Chaotian Chili from Taiwan. Look for it—really! The readily available Huy Fong Food brand works nicely, too.

CHAPTER 1

AMERICAN FISH

AMERICAN FISH

The recipes here are no more "American" than the more clearly identifiably regional recipes in the rest of the book. (What's more American than Latin-influenced food, after all?) I've designated the recipes in this chapter as American because they are more or less what I think of as eclectic American cooking or, as in the case of ahi poke, shrimp and grits, or New England chowder, specific to the history of an American place.

You won't need exotic ingredients to cook the food in this chapter—just fresh fish and herbs, plenty of good greens for cooking and eating raw, and some stellar dairy products like high quality cream (*not* ultrapasteurized), butter, and some really fresh, rather expensive olive oil.

DRINKS

This food calls out for white wine, rosé, or beer. Aside from the obvious universal advice that white wine and seafood go together, if the seafood has some sweetness—cod, lobster, scallops—look for more body and richness in your white wine and a bit less acid. A South African or New Zealand dry Riesling might work nicely—or maybe a very lightly oaked or an unoaked Chardonnay, rather than, say, a highly acidic New Zealand Sauvignon Blanc. That said, you might chill a bottle of Champagne for the Lobster and Black Truffle Linguine (page 61; you may as well lay out a little cash for the wine to pair with that meal).

AT THE TABLE

I'm all about pacing my meal. When it comes time to sit down, especially if you have guests, consider serving a first course. It need not be heavy—a light soup, cold or hot, or a composed salad. If you've been shopping at a fabulous fish store, a first course of raw scallops, thinly sliced and drizzled with olive oil, a few capers, a squeeze of lemon, and a pinch of coarse salt is refreshingly light. Whatever you serve, I always find a first course extends the meal in the best possible way, giving everyone time to sit and talk without the inevitable sense of impending departure that comes with dessert.

One of the great pleasures of cooking well is sitting down to a beautifully set table. There's a lot to be said for cloth napkins, pretty plates, a few candles, and a bouquet of flowers. Don't forget to offer everyone flaky or coarse salt and fresh black pepper. Finish with a crispy sourdough baguette or a loaf of hearty whole-grain levain paired with sweet butter. This is my idea of a perfectly set table.

SWEETS

I'm a baker who loves to toss together dessert. A summer favorite? The most tender shortcakes, piled high with berries or peaches and plenty of whipped cream. When I run out of time before I've gotten to dessert, I know I can rely on my secret stash of excellent chocolate to offer up (Mast Brothers with almonds and sea salt is tops). Open a bag of store-bought cookies (I confess to a weakness for Pepperidge Farm Bordeaux), one more bottle of red wine (or reach for the Port), and call it a night.

NEW ENGLAND COD CHOWDER
WITH BLUE CORN GRIDDLE CAKES AND CHERRY TOMATO—PARSLEY SALAD

SERVES 4

For two centuries New Englanders survived, and happily thrived, by consuming great quantities of salt cod. That was back when the fish was abundant from Cape Cod to Nova Scotia. This chowder, made from cod that's been dried and salted the same way it has been for ages, is profoundly delicious. Each bite has a depth of flavor and meaty texture that's impossible to get in a soup made with fresh fish. Plan ahead. You'll need to soak the fish for a few days to leach the salt out before cooking. It's worth the trouble.

12 OZ/340 G SALT COD

1 TBSP BUTTER

1 SWEET ONION, SUCH AS VIDALIA, COARSELY CHOPPED

2 LARGE YUKON GOLD POTATOES, THINLY SLICED

2 CUPS/480 ML WHOLE MILK

2 CUPS/480 ML HEAVY CREAM

1/2 CUP/20 G CELERY LEAVES, LIGHTLY CHOPPED

FLAKY OR COARSE SALT AND BLACK PEPPER

BUTTER FOR SERVING

Soak the salt cod in cold water for 2 to 3 days in the refrigerator, changing the water each day. Or, if you haven't planned ahead, soak the fish for 5 hours, rinse, and then break the fillets up into pieces. Soak again until you're ready to use it, changing the water frequently. When using salt cod, don't add salt to your recipe until the end.

In a large, heavy pot with a tight-fitting lid, melt the butter over low heat. Add the onion and cook until soft, about 15 minutes, stirring often. When the onion is soft and only just beginning to show a little color on the edges, add the cod, potatoes, and just enough water to cover and cook, tightly covered, for 1 hour over low heat. After 1 hour remove the lid and add the milk and cream. Cook, uncovered, for another 15 minutes over low heat, stirring frequently. To finish, add the celery leaves and taste, adjusting the seasoning with salt and black pepper. (If you want decadence—who doesn't?—add a scrape of butter to each serving bowl.)

FISH NOTE:

There's no substitute for salt cod, but there are various grades. Most important, look for pure white, thick pieces. Norway, Iceland, and Spain still produce a great deal of salt cod; many swear by the quality of the Norwegian product. If you buy your salt cod from a reputable fish store, you'll likely end up with the good stuff. The best of the best is graded "superior extra." Look for superior grade or imperial. Salt cod is sometimes called *morue*, *bacalao*, or saltfish.

— BLUE CORN GRIDDLE CAKES —

Like pancakes, these tasty little cakes are irresistible. Make a big stack and keep them hot by swaddling them in a dish towel and popping them in a warm oven until you're ready to eat. Be sure to have plenty of salted butter on hand.

2 EGGS, AT ROOM TEMPERATURE

1/4 CUP/50 G SUGAR

1 CUP/240 ML WHOLE MILK

5 TBSP/70 G BUTTER, MELTED

1 CUP/140 G BLUE CORNMEAL (SUBSTITUTE YELLOW OR WHITE)

1/2 CUP/65 G ALL-PURPOSE FLOUR

1 TSP KOSHER SALT

1 TSP BAKING SODA

BUTTER FOR THE GRIDDLE

FLAKY OR COARSE SALT

Preheat the oven to 175°F/80°C. Whisk together the eggs and sugar in a large mixing bowl until they lighten in color and appear foamy. Add the milk, then the butter, and mix. Add the cornmeal, flour, kosher salt, and baking soda and then mix with a rubber spatula until the dry ingredients are just incorporated, stirring the batter gently.

Heat a cast-iron griddle or large frying pan and melt 1 tsp of butter on it before adding about 1/3 cup/75 ml of the batter. Do a test cake to be sure the griddle is hot enough. Cook the cakes on the first side until the bubbles settle and the cake is nicely browned. Flip and cook just until crisp. Sprinkle with a little flaky or coarse salt before wrapping the cooked cakes in a clean dish towel and placing them in the warm oven. If the griddle smokes, turn the heat down. Repeat, adding butter as needed and using all the batter.

— CHERRY TOMATO—PARSLEY SALAD —

Look for parsley that is a little softer and smaller than the giant parsley that passes for normal at grocery stores these days. Farmers' markets or your own garden are a good place to start. Make this salad with Sun Gold tomatoes and young, tender parsley and you'll be in for a superior treat.

1 TBSP DIJON MUSTARD

2 TBSP VERY GOOD EXTRA-VIRGIN OLIVE OIL

1 TBSP WHITE OR RED WINE VINEGAR

1 TBSP SHALLOT, MINCED

½ TSP KOSHER SALT

2 PT/680 G CHERRY TOMATOES, PREFERABLY SUN GOLD, HALVED

3 CUPS/120 G FRESH PARSLEY SPRIGS, STEMMED AND SEPARATED INTO SMALL SPRIGS

FLAKY OR COARSE SALT AND BLACK PEPPER

Mix together the mustard, olive oil, vinegar, shallot, and kosher salt in a small bowl. Set aside. Put the tomatoes and parsley in a serving bowl and toss with the dressing just before serving. Add a generous grind of black pepper and a pinch of flaky or coarse salt.

PANFRIED PACIFIC SARDINES,
BALSAMIC ONIONS WITH PEARS, AND
ROASTED FINGERLING POTATOES

SERVES 4

Sweet pears, caramelized onions, and potent sardines are a
fantastic combination; like all great combinations, the whole
surpasses the parts. Add a creamy roasted fingerling potato
to the mix, draped with a few of those onions, and you've got
yourself a quick but most enviable plate.

1 CUP/130 G ALL-PURPOSE FLOUR	4 TO 6 TBSP/55 TO 85 G BUTTER
½ TSP KOSHER SALT	FLAKY OR COARSE SALT
¼ TSP CAYENNE	BALSAMIC ONIONS WITH PEARS (RECIPE FOLLOWS)
16 TO 20 FRESH SARDINES, SCALED AND GUTTED, HEADS LEFT ON	ROASTED FINGERLING POTATOES (RECIPE FOLLOWS)

Combine the flour, kosher salt, and cayenne in a mixing bowl. Dredge
the fish in the flour mixture, coating both sides. Melt 3 tbsp
of the butter in a large frying pan over high heat. When the butter
bubbles and begins to color on the edges, lay the fish in the pan
and cook for 2 to 5 minutes on each side, until brown and crispy.
The fish should not be touching; work in batches or get two pans
going at once. Transfer the fish to a plate and sprinkle with flaky
or coarse salt. Cover loosely with foil to keep warm or set in a
warm oven (175°F/80°C). Repeat to cook the remaining fish. Add additional butter to the pan, as needed.

To serve, lay down a bed of Balsamic Onions on the center of each plate, with sliced pears on top, and then four fish over that. Tuck a few of the Roasted Fingerling Potatoes around the edge and bring to the table.

— BALSAMIC ONIONS WITH PEARS —

Cooking down a couple of sweet onions with balsamic vinegar thrown in toward the end of the process makes for caramelized onions with vim.

2 TBSP OLIVE OIL	2 TBSP BALSAMIC VINEGAR
2 SWEET ONIONS, SUCH AS VIDALIA, THINLY SLICED	2 ANJOU OR BARTLETT PEARS
1 TSP KOSHER SALT	

In a large frying pan over low heat, combine the olive oil, onions, and salt. Cook, stirring frequently, for 20 to 25 minutes or until the onions become a soft, light golden colored mass. Add the balsamic vinegar and cook for another 5 minutes or until the liquid has evaporated. The onions should be sweet, a little tangy, and entirely irresistible.

Just before serving, since pears oxidize very quickly, cut the pears in half and core with a melon baller. Cut the pear halves, top to bottom, into thin slices.

— ROASTED FINGERLING POTATOES —

I always feel a little sheepish about putting a "recipe" like
this in my books, but the truth is that too many cooks over-
look the lovely simplicity of roasting fingerling potatoes with
fresh herbs, olive oil, and flaky salt.

1 LB/455 G FINGERLING POTATOES, SUCH AS
RUSSIAN BANANA OR YELLOW FINN

2 TBSP OLIVE OIL

1/2 TSP KOSHER SALT

1/4 CUP/10 G CHOPPED MIXED FRESH HERBS,
INCLUDING PARSLEY, ROSEMARY,
AND THYME

FLAKY OR COARSE SALT

Preheat the oven to 400°F/200°C/gas 6. Fill a large saucepan with cold
water, add the potatoes, and place over high heat. Once the water
comes to a boil, lower the heat to keep the water at a steady simmer
and cook the potatoes for 15 to 20 minutes or until they are tender
but not falling apart. Test a potato by inserting a paring knife.
There should be little resistance. Drain and toss in a large mixing
bowl with oil and kosher salt, coating the potatoes completely. Set
aside the bowl and any remaining oil. Spread out the potatoes on a
baking sheet and roast for 15 to 20 minutes or until the potatoes
are spotted brown. Return the potatoes to the mixing bowl, toss with
herbs, and finish with a pinch of flaky or coarse salt.

KAUAI AHI POKE
WITH SUSHI RICE AND AVOCADO-DAIKON SALAD

SERVES 4

The first (and last) time I was fortunate enough to visit Hawaii, my father rented a house on the beach in a tiny town on Kauai. My son and daughter were still toddlers. We put their chubby, sandy bodies, worn out by salt water and sun, in their beds early. The grown-ups then made a leisurely evening of it starting with an island specialty called ahi poke—a dish made with spectacular local tuna. (*Poke* means "slice" or "cut" in Hawaiian.) The taste of the wasabi, green onion, and a tiny bit of soy sauce, combined with the fresh, meaty taste of the raw tuna, still reminds me of our days there. Make a light meal of this on a hot summer day and be sure to buy the freshest sushi grade tuna. (See Food Safety and Seafood, page 21.)

1½ LB/680 G SUSHI-GRADE YELLOWTAIL TUNA, CUT INTO 1-IN/2.5-CM CUBES

⅓ CUP/75 ML SOY SAUCE

2 TBSP WASABI POWDER OR PASTE

1½ TSP OLIVE OR VEGETABLE OIL

¼ CUP/25 G THINLY SLICED GREEN ONIONS

COARSE OR FLAKY SALT

SUSHI RICE (RECIPE FOLLOWS)

AVOCADO-DAIKON SALAD (RECIPE FOLLOWS)

PICKLED GINGER FOR SERVING

Fill a large mixing bowl with ice and set it in the refrigerator. Once the fish is cut into chunks, place it in a bowl over the ice while you work. In a small mixing bowl thoroughly combine the soy sauce, wasabi, and oil. Add to the fish and toss to coat the pieces thoroughly. Sprinkle the green onions on top and return the bowl to the refrigerator until you're ready to serve. Taste a piece before you portion it out, and add a pinch of coarse or flaky salt to correct the seasoning.

To serve, make equal piles of each of the three components—poke, rice, and salad—on each plate with a little pile of pickled ginger in the center. (I like to eat this meal with chopsticks.)

<u>FISH NOTE:</u>
Look for troll- or pole-caught yellowfin, bigeye, or skipjack from Alaska and the U.S. Atlantic. Never buy bluefin—wild or ranched.

— SUSHI RICE —

You won't really taste the vinegar, but it'll be there. The stickiness of the rice works with chopsticks, which are the best way to eat the whole meal, from fish to salad.

1 CUP/215 G SUSHI RICE, RINSED AND DRAINED

1¼ CUPS/300 ML WATER

2 TBSP RICE VINEGAR

In a saucepan with a tight-fitting lid, combine the rice and water. Set over medium heat and cook for 10 to 15 minutes, or until the water is absorbed and the rice is tender. Add the vinegar to the rice and mix using a fork, fluffing the rice as you work.

— AVOCADO-DAIKON SALAD —

Avocado and radish pair up with raw fish the way strawberries complement cream. This little salad will make your fish and rice into a meal.

1 DAIKON RADISH (10 OZ/280 G; SUBSTITUTE FRENCH BREAKFAST RADISH), TRIMMED, PEELED, AND SHREDDED

¼ TSP KOSHER SALT

2 HASS AVOCADOS, PITTED, PEELED, AND CUT INTO CUBES

COARSE OR FLAKY SALT

In a serving bowl, toss the radish with the kosher salt. Place the avocado in a layer on top. Sprinkle with coarse or flaky salt.

TROUT
WITH LEMON-HORSERADISH CREAM, PROSCIUTTO KALE, AND CRISPY PARSNIP ROUNDS

SERVES 4

Fresh trout always remind me of my childhood house in Aspen, Colorado, where I was born and spent the first decade of my life. My sister, Nicole, and I caught trout from the bridge that spanned Little Woody Creek in front of our house. I'm sure we were the worst fishermen, but even lousy fishermen get lucky. When we caught a fish, my dad would gut it, sauté it in butter until its skin was crispy, and we'd eat it outdoors watching the stream where the fish had been swimming less than an hour before. Most vividly, I recall the gruesome excitement of killing the fish by whacking its slippery, wriggling head on a smooth river rock. Ah, to be eight years old and glimpsing the twisted perversity of life, death, pleasure, and pain—you must kill the fish to put it out of its misery so that you can experience the indescribable appeal of eating what you've captured. That trout was so fine!

½ CUP/120 ML SOUR CREAM

3 TBSP FRESHLY GRATED HORSERADISH OR JARRED HORSERADISH

¼ CUP/10 G CHOPPED FRESH PARSLEY

1 SHALLOT, CHOPPED

1 TBSP FRESH LEMON JUICE

4 WHOLE OR FILLETED TROUT, GUTTED, WITH HEAD AND TAIL LEFT ON IF WHOLE

½ TSP KOSHER SALT

3 TBSP BUTTER

FLAKY OR COARSE SALT

BLACK PEPPER

To make the sauce, in a small, pretty bowl combine the sour cream, horseradish, parsley, shallot, and lemon juice. Mix well and set aside or refrigerate if more than 1 hour from serving.

Rinse the fish in cold water, dry, and salt both inside and out with kosher salt. Melt the butter in two large sauté pans over medium-high heat. When the butter is hot, lay the fish in the pans on one side. Cook for 3 to 5 minutes, or until the skin is beginning to brown. Move the fish around occasionally by shaking the pan so they don't stick. The butter will brown and smoke a little—don't worry. Flip the trout and cook the other side. Test for doneness by inserting a sharp paring knife in the fish at its thickest point, just behind the head. If the knife slips right in, the fish is done. If you meet some resistance and the fish is well browned and crispy, transfer to an ovenproof plate. Preheat the oven to 200°F/95°C and finish cooking. Test with a knife again before serving. Sprinkle with a pinch of flaky or coarse salt and plenty of black pepper.

FISH NOTE:
Most trout today are farmed in the United States and the European Union. Look for fresh, shiny, bright-eyed specimens. Substitute any other whole saltwater or freshwater fish.

— PROSCIUTTO KALE —

Prosciutto with kale is a winning combination. Served with trout, it's splendid.

2 TBSP OLIVE OIL

1 SMALL SHALLOT, CHOPPED (ABOUT 1 TBSP)

1 LB/455 G KALE, RINSED, DRIED, STEMMED, AND COARSELY CHOPPED

2 TBSP WATER

1/4 TSP KOSHER SALT

2 OZ/55 G PROSCIUTTO, CUT INTO LONG THREADS

In your largest, deepest frying pan, heat the oil with the shallot over medium heat. When the oil shimmers, add the kale and water. Use tongs to turn the unwieldy greens over, slowly coating them with oil to prevent the bottoms from burning. The kale will quickly wilt, making it more manageable as you continue to cook for 5 to 7 minutes. I like my kale just wilted and heated through. Add the prosciutto to just heat it once the kale is cooked to your taste.

— CRISPY PARSNIP ROUNDS —

Underused and underappreciated, parsnips have a complex flavor
with a sweetness that makes them perfect candidates for carameliz-
ing. Butter, salt, and a long, slow cook are all it takes to get most
of these little rounds crispy, while others remain soft.

2 TBSP BUTTER

1 LB/455 G PARSNIPS, PEELED AND THINLY SLICED

3 SPRIGS FRESH THYME

1/4 TSP KOSHER SALT

In a large frying pan over medium-low heat, combine the butter,
parsnips, thyme, and salt. Cook, stirring frequently, for 20 to
25 minutes or until the parsnips have colored and most have
become crispy. Some will blacken in spots while others may
remain soft. Don't worry; they'll all be delicious!

BACON-WRAPPED GRILLED TROUT,

WALNUT LENTILS, AND SAUTÉED BABY KALE WITH APPLE

SERVES 4

Trout is to bacon as gin is to cucumber. Likewise, lentils and
walnuts are uncannily good together—as are apples and kale.
Cooking a fish wrapped in bacon is easy because the fish
won't stick to the grill or dry out.

1 TSP KOSHER SALT

4 WHOLE TROUT, GUTTED, HEADS AND TAILS LEFT ON

1 LB/455 G THINLY SLICED BACON

BLACK PEPPER

¼ CUP/10 G CHOPPED FRESH PARSLEY

Salt the interior of the trout. Begin wrapping the bacon around
the fish from the gills down, leaving the head uncovered and
overlapping the slices slightly to give the fish complete, secure
coverage. You can tuck the final strip under or keep it in place
with a toothpick.

Clean and oil the grates of your grill thoroughly. Build a medium
fire in a charcoal or wood grill or preheat a gas grill to medium.
Put the trout on the hottest part of the grill and cook for about
5 minutes a side or until the bacon is crispy. Watch for flare-ups
as the fat drips, but don't worry if there are some black spots.
Trust me, it'll all be tasty. Unless the trout is very large, the fish
should be cooked when the bacon is crispy. If you're concerned, a
thermometer inserted just behind the head, at the thickest point
on the fish, should read 135 to 140°F/57 to 60°C.

Watch for bones. I recommend serving the fish whole and advising everyone to unwrap it, gently remove the top fillet with a fork and then, lifting from the head, remove the spine right down to the tail. Put a bone dish on the table and everyone will be happy.

<u>FISH NOTE:</u>
Most trout today are farm raised, either in the United States or the European Union. They're a good, sustainable choice. If you prefer not to use trout, feel free to substitute almost any other whole fish. You might consider porgy (scup) or snapper from a sustainable source.

— WALNUT LENTILS —

I eat lentils all the time: for breakfast with an egg on top, for lunch with a few greens, and for dinner with whatever bit of protein happens to be on my plate. Double this recipe and see what you think of a lentil-obsessed existence.

1 CUP/220 G FRENCH PUY LENTILS

2½ CUPS/600 G CHICKEN OR FISH STOCK (PAGE 27) OR WATER

KOSHER SALT

¾ CUP/100 G WALNUTS, TOASTED (SEE PAGE 30), SALTED, AND COARSELY CHOPPED

In a medium saucepan, combine the lentils and chicken stock and set over medium heat. Simmer for 25 to 30 minutes, or until the lentils are tender and the liquid is absorbed. As the lentils finish cooking, watch carefully for scorching. Add some salt, stir, and taste, adding more salt as needed. Finish by sprinkling walnuts on top.

— SAUTÉED BABY KALE WITH APPLE —

Don't worry if you can't find baby kale. Instead, use mature kale
with the center stem cut out. Cut the big leaves across into ribbons.

2 TBSP OLIVE OIL

1 SWEET ONION, SUCH AS VIDALIA, CHOPPED

1 GARLIC CLOVE, MINCED

1/4 TSP KOSHER SALT

1 APPLE (I LIKE GRANNY SMITH, JONAGOLD, AND PINK LADY)

10 OZ/280 G BABY KALE, RINSED AND DRIED

FLAKY OR COARSE SALT

In a large sauté pan, heat the oil over medium heat. Add the onion
and cook for 5 to 7 minutes, stirring frequently. Add the garlic and
kosher salt. Cook for 2 to 3 minutes or until the onion is soft.
Using the large holes on a standard-size grater, shred the apple
directly into the pan, skin and all, leaving just the core and seeds
behind. Add the kale, stirring as you do so to speed the wilting of
the leaves so they can all fit into the pan. Once all the kale is
in, increase the heat to high and cook for 3 to 5 minutes or until
the greens are soft and the apple has given up some of its moisture. Without overcooking the greens, let some of the moisture cook
away before removing the pan from the heat. Add a pinch of flaky
or coarse salt to finish.

NEW HAVEN WHITE CLAM PIE
AND BEET-FETA SALAD

SERVES 4

Just because you can't get to New Haven, Connecticut, doesn't mean you shouldn't get to taste this astounding pizza. Don't be intimidated about making your own pie—it couldn't be easier. All you need are really fresh clams, plus a ball of pizza dough, either bought— try asking your local pizza joint for the dough they use for a large pie—or homemade. Olive oil, herbs, and a bit of prosciutto or bacon, and you'll be biting into something spectacular.

PIZZA DOUGH

$1\frac{1}{2}$ CUPS/360 ML WARM (NOT HOT) WATER

1 TSP INSTANT YEAST

1 TBSP KOSHER SALT

1 TSP SUGAR

$\frac{1}{4}$ CUP/60 ML OLIVE OIL, PLUS MORE FOR OILING YOUR HANDS AND THE DOUGH

3 CUPS/385 G UNBLEACHED ALL-PURPOSE FLOUR, PLUS MORE FOR WORKING THE DOUGH

$\frac{1}{2}$ CUP/65 G WHOLE-WHEAT OR SEMOLINA FLOUR

OLIVE OIL FOR THE PAN AND (OPTIONAL) WORK SURFACE

ALL-PURPOSE FLOUR FOR THE WORK SURFACE IF NOT USING OIL

ONE $1\frac{1}{2}$-LB/680-G BALL STORE-BOUGHT PIZZA DOUGH (IF YOU'RE NOT MAKING YOUR OWN)

1 HEAD GARLIC, CLOVES PEELED AND CHOPPED

$\frac{1}{4}$ CUP/60 ML VERY GOOD EXTRA-VIRGIN OLIVE OIL

2 TBSP CHOPPED FRESH BASIL

2 TBSP CHOPPED FRESH PARSLEY

2 TBSP CHOPPED FRESH OREGANO

2 TBSP FRESH THYME LEAVES

50 CLAMS, LITTLENECK OR CHERRYSTONE

1 CUP/240 ML DRY WHITE WINE

2 OZ/55 G THINLY SLICED PROSCIUTTO OR COOKED BACON, RIPPED INTO SMALL PIECES

$\frac{1}{4}$ CUP/30 G GRATED PARMESAN

To make the pizza dough: Mix together the water, yeast, salt, and sugar in the bowl of a stand mixer, or in a mixing bowl if working by hand. Add the olive oil, all-purpose flour, and whole-wheat flour (or use all white flour if you prefer). If using a stand mixer, attach a dough hook and work at medium speed for 5 minutes. If you're working by hand, use a wooden spoon to mix the flour, and then turn the dough out onto a clean, lightly floured surface. Oil your hands and work the dough, kneading until you have a cohesive ball and the dough is elastic. Whichever method you're using, oil your hands, coat the dough, and place in a well-oiled bowl. Let sit at room temperature for 1 to 2 hours. If the dough is very sticky at this point, use oil rather than flour to work with it. Either way, punch down the dough and turn it out onto a clean surface.

Preheat the oven to 500°F/260°C/gas 10. Coat a baking sheet with olive oil. On a lightly floured or oiled work surface, roll out the pizza dough into a large rectangle and transfer to a baking sheet. Use your rolling pin or hands to press the dough to fit the pan. Set aside to rise while you prepare the toppings. Combine the garlic and olive oil in a small bowl. Mix the four kinds of herbs together in another small bowl and divide them in half. Put half in with the garlic and oil. Reserve the other half for garnishing the pizza once it is out of the oven.

Rinse the clams under cold water, discarding any that are open or damaged. Put the clams in a large pot with a tight-fitting lid, add the wine, cover, and cook over medium heat for 10 minutes or until the clams are open just enough to put your index finger between the two shells. Turn off the heat and drain the clams in a colander. (Reserve the liquid to rinse the clams or to combine with the liquor from the clams and use for chowder or pasta!) Use a butter knife or a clam or oyster shucking tool to open the clams the rest of the way. Remove the meat from the clams, reserving the liquor in a separate bowl. The clams should still be quite raw. Don't worry if you tear them. If they are very sandy, rinse in the cooking liquid.

Spread the garlic and herb mixture evenly over the surface of the pizza, coating the dough all the way to the edge. Scatter the clams and the prosciutto over the surface. Bake for 8 to 12 minutes or until the pizza is crusty brown on the edges. Sprinkle the Parmesan and reserved herbs over the surface and bring the pizza to the table whole.

FISH NOTE:
The most common clams you'll find at the market are farmed quahog clams, often called littlenecks. Cherrystones are just the smaller of these ubiquitous hard-shells. You'll also find manila clams, and the East Coast soft-shell, often called steamer clams. Any variety will work for this pizza. Look for tightly closed clams with no chips, cracks, or slime on the shell.

— BEET-FETA SALAD —

Piquant and yet sweet, this salad is a lovely complement to the clam pie. Think of it as a relish that's meant to be eaten right alongside the pie.

2 LARGE RED BEETS (ABOUT 14 OZ/400 G TOTAL), SCRUBBED

2 LARGE GOLDEN BEETS (ABOUT 14 OZ/400 G TOTAL), SCRUBBED

1 TBSP OLIVE OIL

1 TBSP WATER

1/4 TSP KOSHER SALT

2 TBSP VERY GOOD EXTRA-VIRGIN OLIVE OIL

1 TSP WHITE WINE VINEGAR

FLAKY OR COARSE SALT

3 1/2 OZ/100 G FETA (I LIKE THE FRENCH-MADE VALBRESO)

Preheat the oven to 350°F/180°C/gas 4. Place a large sheet of foil on a baking sheet. Lay the beets in the center, sprinkle on the tbsp of olive oil, the water, and the kosher salt. Lay a second sheet of foil on top and then crimp the edges of the two sheets together to make a tightly sealed package. Bake the beets for 40 minutes or until tender. If the skins are tough, they will slip off; if not, leave them on and eat them.

Slice the beets crosswise, and then cut each slice in half. Place the beets in a serving bowl and toss with the extra-virgin olive oil and vinegar. Sprinkle with a bit of flaky or coarse salt and then crumble the feta on top.

SHRIMP,
GRITS, SHRIMP BUTTER, AND GREENS

SERVES 4

Edna Lewis, the doyenne of Southern cooking, is the inspiration
for this classic combination. I love her shrimp paste, which she
grew up putting on grits. I've followed her lead, and then layered
on shrimp, greens, a soft-cooked egg, and finally green onions. It's
one plate, and it's *good*. How delicious this dish is depends in no
small part on the freshness and quality of your shrimp. Buy from
a trusted fish shop, and you'll taste the difference in sweetness.
Have your Grits, Shrimp Butter, and Greens ready to go before you
start cooking the shrimp.

3 TBSP BUTTER

1 LB/455 G SHRIMP, PEELED, DEVEINED, AND
HALVED LENGTHWISE (5 TO 8 SHRIMP PER PLATE,
DEPENDING ON SIZE)

1 JALAPEÑO CHILE, MINCED, OR 1 TBSP SMOKY
SWEET HOT SAUCE (PAGE 211)

4 EGGS, PREFERABLY ORGANIC

FLAKY OR COARSE SALT AND BLACK PEPPER

GRITS (RECIPE FOLLOWS)

SHRIMP BUTTER (RECIPE FOLLOWS)

GREENS (RECIPE FOLLOWS)

6 GREEN ONIONS, WHITE AND TENDER
GREEN PARTS, SLICED

In a large frying pan set over high heat, melt 2 tbsp of the butter
until it foams, add the shrimp and jalapeño, and sauté for 3 to
5 minutes, or until the shrimp color and curl. Don't overcook—once
they've curled up, they're done. Melt the remaining 1 tbsp of butter
in the frying pan (no need to wash it) over medium-low heat. Crack
the eggs into the hot butter and fry them until the whites are firm
(sunny-side up). Add a generous pinch of salt and a grind of pepper.
To plate, lay down a layer of Grits on one side of the plate, followed by a good dollop of the Shrimp Butter. Put the Greens opposite, and the shrimp on top of the Grits. Top with the egg. Sprinkle
everything with green onions.

FISH NOTE:
Wild-caught shrimp and farmed in the United States are the best
choices, with wild spot prawns from Alaska and wild pink shrimp
from Oregon being the best of the best. Avoid: farm-raised
shrimp from Asia, including those from China, India, Thailand,
and Malaysia.

— GRITS —

Stone-ground grits are the holy grail of corn products in the
South. They have a bigger, nuttier, sweeter corn flavor and a more
toothsome texture than commercially produced grits that you buy
at the grocery store in the North. That said, Bob's Red Mill makes
pretty good grits. But the most incredible grits I've tasted are
Anson Mills white grits from Columbia, South Carolina. Their flavor
is so pronounced, they remind me of creamed corn. I generally don't
like my grits made with milk, but if you do, don't let my heretical,
non-Southern opinion keep you off your dairy.

8 CUPS/2 L WATER, PLUS MORE AS NEEDED   2 CUPS/280 G GRITS

2 TSP KOSHER SALT

In a large saucepan set over medium heat, combine the water, kosher
salt, and grits. Whisk and cook for 30 to 40 minutes. Turn down the
heat as the grits thicken, adding more water if necessary. You
want the grits nice and thick—the bubbles should make a messy
explosion on the surface. Taste for salt, remembering that you'll
be buttering them up with the Shrimp Butter, which is both salty
and spicy.

— SHRIMP BUTTER —

"Paste" is a word made for a dentist or a mason. I prefer "butter"—
who wouldn't? Sorry, Edna. You're no less of a genius.

½ CUP/115 G BUTTER

8 OZ/225 G SHRIMP, PEELED AND DEVEINED

¼ TSP CAYENNE PEPPER

½ TSP SALT

BLACK PEPPER

⅓ CUP/75 ML FINO SHERRY

2 TBSP FRESH LEMON JUICE

In a medium frying pan set over medium heat, melt 2 tbsp of butter
until foaming, add the shrimp, and sauté for 3 to 5 minutes or until
the shrimp color and curl. Use tongs to transfer the shrimp to the
bowl of a food processor.

Add another 3 tbsp of butter to the hot pan along with the cayenne,
salt, plenty of freshly ground black pepper, Sherry, and lemon
juice. Simmer over medium heat for about 3 minutes. The mixture
should be fragrant and have reduced slightly. Pour the hot liquid
into the food processor bowl with the shrimp and blend, using the
blade attachment, for 1 full minute. Stop the machine and use a
rubber spatula to scrape down the sides. Pulse for another minute
and then add the remaining 3 tbsp of butter. Blend for another
minute, transfer to a ramekin or small bowl, and place in the
refrigerator to firm up before you use it. (This isn't strictly
necessary, since it will melt on the grits anyway, but do refrigerate it in any case, if you have the time.)

— GREENS —

It might just be because I'm a girl, but sautéed kale with plenty of garlic is one of my favorite foods. Use any variety of greens you like—collards would be traditional, beet greens would be lovely, mustard splendid. Just use your judgment and cook until tender without letting the pan go dry.

2 TBSP OLIVE OIL

½ HEAD GARLIC, CLOVES PEELED AND THINLY SLICED

1 OR 2 LARGE BUNCHES OF GREENS, RINSED AND RIBBED AS NEEDED

½ TSP KOSHER SALT

¼ CUP/60 ML WATER, PLUS MORE AS NEEDED

FLAKY OR COARSE SALT

In a large frying pan or wok, heat the oil briefly over medium-low heat. Add the garlic, greens, kosher salt, and water and cook, turning the greens with tongs or a spatula, for 5 to 8 minutes, until the greens are wilted and tender. Add additional water if the pan is dry and the greens begin to stick. Keep the heat low so you don't brown the garlic. Sprinkle with a pinch of flaky or coarse salt.

LOBSTER AND BLACK TRUFFLE LINGUINE
WITH SOUR APPLE–BIBB LETTUCE SALAD

SERVES 4

This is a pasta to serve with Champagne on a night when you're feeling celebratory and a bit outrageous. It's full of non-everyday ingredients. That said, it's simple to make. After boiling the lobster, all you need to do is crack its shells and make a simple reduction finished with cream and truffle butter. (I like the D'Artagnan brand.)

2 CUPS/480 ML DRY WHITE WINE, SUCH AS SAUVIGNON BLANC OR UNOAKED CHARDONNAY

1/4 CUP/60 ML DRY VERMOUTH

2 BAY LEAVES

TWO 1 1/2-LB/680-G LIVE MAINE LOBSTERS

3 CARROTS, PEELED AND HALVED LENGTHWISE

1 ONION, PEELED AND QUARTERED

3 LARGE, LEAFY SPRIGS FRESH PARSLEY

3 BUSHY SPRIGS FRESH THYME

1 THUMB-LENGTH PIECE FRESH GINGER, PEELED

3 RIBS CELERY WITH LEAVES, HALVED LENGTHWISE

2 TBSP UNSALTED BUTTER

1 MEDIUM SHALLOT, MINCED

1 LB/455 G MUSHROOMS, SUCH AS MAITAKE, CREMINI, CHANTERELLE, OR A MIX (DO NOT USE PORTOBELLOS OR SHIITAKES)

1 1/2 TO 2 CUPS/360 TO 480 ML HEAVY CREAM

6 TBSP/90 G BLACK TRUFFLE BUTTER (NOT TRUFFLE OIL!)

1 LB/455 G DRIED OR FRESH LINGUINE, COOKED AL DENTE IN UNSALTED WATER

1/4 CUP/10 G CHOPPED FRESH CHERVIL

WHITE PEPPER

Set up a steamer basket in a large stockpot over high heat and fill the stockpot just up to the steamer basket with the wine, vermouth, bay leaves, and water. Set the lobsters in the pot, cover, and steam for 7 to 10 minutes, or until the shells of the lobsters are dappled a deep orange color. Remove the lobsters with tongs and set aside to cool. Once cool enough to handle, crack the shells and pick out the lobster meat, keeping the pieces as large as possible and reserving the shells.

Return the cracked shells to the stockpot, mashing them with a wooden pestle or spoon, or using a cracker to break apart the large pieces of shell. Add the carrots, onion, parsley, thyme, ginger, and celery. Cover the shells and vegetables with water—just—and set over high heat. Bring to a boil, reduce the heat to a simmer, and skim off any scum that rises to the top. Simmer for 1 hour, uncovered, stirring occasionally. Strain the stock and return the liquid to the pot. Set over medium heat and reduce for another 30 minutes, or until there's about 2 cups/480 ml of liquid. Set aside.

To finish the sauce, set a large sauté pan over medium heat with the butter, shallot, and mushrooms. Cook for 5 to 8 minutes, or until the shallot softens and the mushrooms begin to wilt and give up their fragrance. Do not add any salt. Next, add the stock and $1^1/_2$ cups/360 ml cream and reduce by half. Taste the sauce— if it's too salty, add a little more cream. To finish the sauce, add the truffle butter and the reserved lobster meat. Cook just until the butter melts and the lobster is just warm.

Toss the pasta with 1 cup/240 ml of the liquid from the sauce. Portion the pasta into bowls, and then distribute the lobster meat and mushrooms from the bottom of the pan. Finish each portion with a sprinkling of chervil and the faintest bit of white pepper.

FISH NOTE:
Never buy precooked lobsters at the grocery store—they likely died and were then cooked. Grim but true. You can pick out a lively lobster and ask the store to cook it for you, however. Just make sure the lobster you picked out live is the lobster you leave with. Ask for it lightly cooked, 8 to 10 minutes, depending on size. Substitute shrimp if you prefer; make the reduction with the shells and heads, if you have them.

— SOUR APPLE—BIBB LETTUCE SALAD —

A simple salad with a bracing acidity to eat after this rich meal.
It'll cleanse your palate and get you ready for a bite of cheese.
Superfresh lettuce is sweet and flavorful.

1 GRANNY SMITH OR OTHER TART APPLE

1 TSP FRESH LEMON JUICE

1 TO 2 HEADS BIBB LETTUCE

1 TBSP VERY GOOD EXTRA-VIRGIN OLIVE OIL

FLAKY OR COARSE SALT AND BLACK PEPPER

Peel the apple and cut it into uniform cubes the width of your
pinky nail. As you work, place them in the bottom of a small bowl
and toss with the lemon juice to coat. Rip the lettuce leaves into
manageable pieces—maybe in quarters, depending on their size—and
place them in a salad bowl. Toss the lettuce with the olive oil, a
pinch of salt, and a grind of black pepper. Scatter the apple pieces
on top and you're done.

SQUID, FRIED EGG, FRESH HERB, AND WALNUT SPAGHETTI
WITH PEAR-ARUGULA SALAD

SERVES 4

Squid, with their toothsome consistency, go beautifully here with the soft egg, the bright herbs, and the rich nuts. If you've never made a pasta of this sort at home, it's time. This is a forgiving, fast meal. Use the ingredients you have on hand—different kinds of nuts, herbs from the garden, greens, vegetables. Sauté them with olive oil and, unless you prefer to follow the Italian rule of no cheese with seafood, shower with Parmesan or another cheese, such as ricotta salata or pecorino. In other words, break the rules and open a decent bottle of red wine to see you on your way.

4 GARLIC CLOVES, MINCED

2 ANCHOVY FILLETS, CHOPPED

12 CAPERS

1/4 CUP/60 ML VERY GOOD EXTRA-VIRGIN OLIVE OIL

4 TO 6 CUPS/960 ML TO 1.4 L VEGETABLE OIL

KOSHER SALT

1 1/2 CUPS/170 G DRIED BREAD CRUMBS

1 LB/455 G SQUID TENTACLES (CUT INTO STILL-INTACT, BITE-SIZE CLUSTERS)

4 EGGS, FRIED SUNNY-SIDE UP IN BUTTER OR OLIVE OIL

1 LB/455 G SPAGHETTI OR NOODLES OF YOUR CHOICE, COOKED AL DENTE IN SALTED WATER

1/2 CUP/20 G CHOPPED MIXED FRESH OREGANO, BASIL, AND PARSLEY

1/4 CUP/20 G ITALIAN PINE NUTS (ALWAYS AVOID PINE NUTS FROM CHINA; SEE PAGE 80)

ZEST OF 1/2 LEMON

COARSE OR FLAKY SALT (OPTIONAL) AND BLACK PEPPER

Preheat the oven to 175°F/80°C. In a small saucepan set over very low heat, combine the garlic, anchovies, capers, and olive oil. Heat the oil until hot, and then turn off the heat. Mash the garlic, anchovies, and capers together, and then allow the mixture to sit while you prepare the other ingredients.

Pour the vegetable oil into a large, deep frying pan set over high heat, or pour it into the basin of an electric fryer. The frying pan should have a depth of at least 1/2 in/12 mm of oil. Bring the oil to 350°F/180°C or, if you don't have a thermometer, heat it until it begins to smoke. (Turn the heat off if it smokes and you aren't ready to add the squid.) In a medium mixing bowl combine 1 tsp of kosher salt and the bread crumbs. Coat the squid in the bread crumb mixture and then place them in the hot oil in batches. Cook the squid for 2 to 3 minutes, turning after 1 or 2 minutes to cook the other side. The crumbs should be a nice toasty brown. Transfer the cooked squid to a paper towel-lined plate and give them a little pinch of kosher salt. Set in the warming oven. Cook the eggs, leaving the yolks runny. The pasta should be in the water cooking.

To serve the pasta, toss the spaghetti with the oil-garlic mixture. Portion out the spaghetti into four bowls. Distribute the squid, put an egg on top of each serving, scatter the herbs over the egg, and then the pine nuts and a bit of lemon zest. A grind of black pepper and possibly a pinch of flaky or coarse salt finishes it. The egg should be chopped so its runny yolk becomes part of the sauce—but I like to let everyone do that themselves at the table.

FISH NOTE:
Longfin squid from the U.S. Atlantic are sustainable and abundant. If you prefer, you could make this recipe with shrimp. Simply follow the instructions as written, and add the shrimp when you would add the squid, cooking them for 3 to 8 minutes, depending on how big they are.

— PEAR-ARUGULA SALAD —

Another elemental salad that shows off the quality of the ingredients more than the cook's skills. That's okay by me. A perfectly ripe pear feels like a gift—too often they're not quite right. Feel the top of the pear (the stem end), which should just yield when the fruit is ripe.

1 RIPE BARTLETT OR ANJOU PEAR	1 TBSP VERY GOOD EXTRA-VIRGIN OLIVE OIL
1 TSP FRESH LEMON JUICE	FLAKY OR COARSE SALT
5 OZ/140 G ARUGULA	3 OZ/85 G ASIAGO FRESCO

Cut the pear in half and remove the core by scooping it out with a spoon or melon baller. Cut away the stem. Without peeling, cut the pear into cubes the width of the nail on your pinky finger. Place them in a small bowl with the lemon juice, tossing to coat as you work. Just before you're ready to eat, put the arugula in a serving bowl and toss it with the olive oil and a pinch of salt. The arugula should be lightly coated and just glistening. Scatter the pear on top, leaving behind the lemon juice. Top with finely shaved Asiago. (Use either a cheese slicer or a vegetable peeler.) Serve the salad in layers, without tossing.

CHAPTER 2

BISTRO FISH

BISTRO FISH

What you'll find in this chapter are recognizable sauces (such as béarnaise) and combinations—fish and chips, mussels with cream and saffron—that we, Americans, identify with Europe. For the most part, this is Old World food. I hope cooking these recipes at home will be the most welcome surprise, as you discover just how good these classics are when you make them yourself using the best ingredients.

You'll need plenty of fresh herbs, a stellar source for vegetables—especially greens and lettuces—plus great dairy and olive oil. Consider investing in a bottle of high quality Champagne or white wine vinegar—one made in France is a good bet. It's surprising how much of a difference these small details make to the flavor of your food. When I work with great cream, for example, even the kids notice that it tastes extra luxurious.

DRINKS

When you're cooking the food in this chapter, I think it makes sense to leave the New World. Reach instead for an understated Sancerre from France's Loire Valley or a Spanish Albariño. Lots of us forget that bubbles aren't just for birthdays—consider Lambrusco. Serve this bright, understated, red and pink bubbly cold. (I know, Lambrusco brings back visions of forgettable sweet wines from the 1970s. This is not that wine, I promise.) Lambrusco is both the grape and the name of the region where this wine is made. Low in alcohol, fruity, and easy to quaff, this wine will see you through recipes that are rich, spicy, and assertive. Wine critic for the *New York Times*, Eric Asimov, has a terrific column on Lambrusco if you want some more tips. His favorite: Lambrusco Grasparossa di Castelvetro Pruno Nero from Cleto Chiarli.

AT THE TABLE

Pace yourself when you're eating European food by following a French rhythm. Dream up a simple first course, follow with your main course, but save the salad for after the meal, to pair up with some cheese. This is the best way to facilitate that essential practice of lingering at the table. There are few things in life so worthwhile and the French—among others—have sitting long at the table down to an effortless art.

Virtually every recipe in this chapter would benefit from a crusty loaf of sourdough bread to pass around. Locate the best baker in your shopping circumference. Taste and test and ask around. Who doesn't lust after flavorful, chewy bread smeared with fresh, sweet butter?

SWEETS

The best way to follow many of these rich meals is with a perfectly ripe cheese (a stinky Reblochon is never a disappointment), seasonal fruit, and some high quality dark chocolate. If you haven't had a salad, put it out at the same time but keep it simple, like Tossed Greens (page 77). If you'd rather be extravagant or if you're really in the mood to do it up right, serve cheese and then go to a stunning dessert like vacherin—meringue with ice cream. Go daring with ice cream—salted caramel or bing cherry—and make it yourself out of the best ingredients. Serve with a fresh raspberry coulis or dark chocolate sauce sprinkled with the merest bit of flaky sea salt.

BEER BATTER-FRIED FISH AND CHIPS
WITH TARTAR SAUCE, RASPBERRY VINEGAR SHRUB, AND PUB SALAD

SERVES 4

Is deep-frying a hassle? Definitely. Is it worth the trouble? Fry up some cod in this beer batter to see if you regret it. Making fish and chips with beer batter isn't just a gimmick—beer adds flavor and a lightness you don't get any other way. The results? Crispy fish that pairs up with the Chips, Tartar Sauce, and Raspberry Vinegar Shrub like nothing you've ever tasted.

1 TO 2 GAL/3.8 TO 7.5 L PEANUT OR VEGETABLE OIL

2 CUPS/255 G FLOUR

KOSHER SALT

1/4 TSP CAYENNE PEPPER

2 CUPS/480 ML LAGER, PILSNER, OR WHEAT BEER

FOUR 8-OZ/225-G COD FILLETS

1 LEMON, CUT INTO 8 WEDGES

CHIPS (RECIPE FOLLOWS)

TARTAR SAUCE (RECIPE FOLLOWS)

RASPBERRY VINEGAR SHRUB (RECIPE FOLLOWS)

Pour the oil into a large a stockpot or deep fryer. Turn up the heat to high, and bring the oil to 375°F/190°C. In a mixing bowl combine the flour, 1 tsp of salt, and the cayenne. When you're ready to fry the fish, add the beer to the flour mixture and whisk to combine into a smooth batter.

Dip the cod in the batter, turning so each fillet is well coated. Carefully lower the fish into the hot oil in batches, and cook until the coating is a deep golden brown, 6 to 8 minutes. Transfer the fish to a paper towel-lined plate or to a cooling rack, sprinkle with more salt, and eat while the fish is hot and crispy. Serve with lemon wedges, Chips, Tartar Sauce, and shrub.

FISH NOTE:
Buy Pacific cod or North Atlantic cod (from Nova Scotia), Pacific
haddock, or, for a supersustainable choice, U.S. farmed catfish.
Avoid: Catfish farmed in Asia.

— CHIPS —

I recommend using a large stockpot for frying. It gives you some
cover if the oil boils up, and it gives you the ability to control
the heat, since you're working on the stove top you know (and love?).

Since you're frying the fish anyway, none of this is a big deal.
You've gotten the place greasy anyway, so why not throw in some
potatoes? They sure taste good in that tartar sauce, not to mention
dipped in a little of that shrub. Besides, who doesn't love calling
fries "chips," as if we always call them that.

5 LARGE RUSSET POTATOES, PEELED AND SET IN
A BOWL OF COLD WATER

1 TO 2 GAL/3.8 TO 7.5 L PEANUT OR VEGETABLE OIL

KOSHER SALT

If you love your mandoline, use it to cut the potatoes into thin
slices and then into strips to make skinny fries. If you and your
mandoline don't speak or possibly haven't met, just cut your
potatoes with a knife into the most even strips you can manage.
In either case, put the strips in a large bowl full of water as
you work. In a perfect world you will let the potatoes soak for
a few hours to leech out some of the starch so that they fry up
super-crispy. Changing the water once or twice helps get that
starch out, too.

Preheat the oven to 200°F/95°C. Pour the oil into a large stockpot
or deep fryer set over high heat. Bring the oil to 330°F/165°C or heat
until it just shimmers and moves. This is the temperature for the
first round only.

To make the chips, you're going to cook them twice. I know, it's a
pain but it's worth it to get them crispy and light. Working in
batches, dry the potato pieces and fry them for 5 minutes. They
should not brown.

Drain the half-cooked fries on a rack or on a baking sheet lined with paper towels. Turn the heat up under the pot and bring the oil to the point of being dangerously hot or just shy of its smoke point, at least 375°F/190°C. Again working in batches, cook the fries for 8 to 10 minutes or until they are a lovely nut brown. Transfer to clean paper towels or a rack and salt generously. Keep the fries hot in the warm oven until you're ready to eat—which is better sooner than later when it comes to "chips."

— TARTAR SAUCE —

I can't taste the sweet, rich, gentle tartness of Tartar Sauce without being transported to the crispy, burn-your-tongue-hot fish sticks I slathered it on as a kid when my parents went out to dinner.

1 CUP/240 ML MAYONNAISE, FULL FAT

2 TBSP RELISH OR MINCED GHERKINS OR SWEET PICKLES

1 TBSP FRESH LEMON JUICE

1 EGG YOLK

BLACK PEPPER

In a small, pretty serving bowl mix together the mayonnaise, relish, lemon juice, egg yolk, and black pepper. Taste, and add a little more relish or lemon juice, depending on whether you prefer it sweet or sour.

— RASPBERRY VINEGAR SHRUB —

Have no fear: a shrub is just a vinegar-based drink. I've made this one strong, more like the base for a shrub. If you want to drink it and use it as a condiment, add some to a glass of bubbly water. It's almost like drinking kombucha.

½ CUP/120 ML MALT VINEGAR

10 FRESH RASPBERRIES, GENTLY MASHED

Combine the raspberries with the vinegar in a small bowl or pitcher. Stir and let sit for 30 minutes.

— PUB SALAD —

This unassuming little salad takes some planning because it's composed almost entirely of pickles. Make them a day ahead and then make the salad. If that's not going to happen, let the eggs and beets pickle for at least an hour.

2 BEETS, TRIMMED, PEELED, AND QUARTERED

2 HARD-BOILED EGGS, PEELED

1 CUP/240 ML CIDER VINEGAR

1 LARGE BUNCH WATERCRESS, RINSED AND BROKEN INTO MANAGEABLE STEMS

1 TBSP OLIVE OIL

FLAKY OR COARSE SALT

Place a steamer basket in a medium saucepan with a tight-fitting lid and fill the bottom of the pot with water. Place the beets in the basket, cover, and set the pot over high heat. Cook for 30 to 35 minutes or until the beets are tender. Test by inserting a knife into the center of the largest piece. If there is no resistance, they're done. Put the pieces in a 1-qt/960-ml size mason jar or other heat-proof container with a lid. Put the eggs in the same jar. Give the beet pot a quick rinse and use it to bring the vinegar to a boil. Pour it over the beets and eggs. Fill the remaining space in the jar with water, screw on the lid, and refrigerate for up to 10 days or at least 1 hour.

To make the salad, put the watercress in a pretty serving bowl—glass would be ideal. Add the olive oil and a pinch of salt and toss. Place the beets on top of the watercress. Using your sharpest knife, cut the eggs from top to bottom into oval slices. Lay them gently on top of the beets. Sprinkle a little salt on the eggs and serve.

BASQUE PEASANT BACALAO:
CHILES, POTATOES, SWEET PEPPERS, AND TOMATOES OVER TOAST WITH TOSSED GREENS

SERVES 4

This is about as good, and as elegant, as hearty peasant food gets. It'll take you 10 minutes to put together, but you need to plan ahead by soaking the fish in water for 3 days in advance. The reward for your foresight? A plate of snow-white cod that's fragrant, fresh, and colorful, with just a hint of spice from the chile. The crisp, buttered toast lining the plate makes the whole dish irresistible. Have a few extra slices of toast handy as an excuse to soak up the last drops of broth.

1 LB/455 G SALT COD

12 OZ/340 G BACON

2 TBSP OLIVE OIL

5 MEDIUM POTATOES, RED OR YELLOW FLESH, CUT INTO THICK SLICES

1 PINT CHERRY TOMATOES, QUARTERED

1 SMALL GREEN BELL PEPPER, SEEDED AND CUT INTO THIN ROUNDS

1 SMALL RED BELL PEPPER, SEEDED AND CUT INTO THIN ROUNDS

1 CHILE, SUCH AS A SERRANO OR JALAPEÑO, WITH ITS SEEDS, SLICED

1 SWEET ONION, SUCH AS VIDALIA, CUT INTO THIN ROUNDS

4 SLICES LEVAIN OR OTHER HEARTY, FLAVORFUL BREAD, PLUS MORE FOR THE TABLE

4 TO 6 TBSP/55 TO 85 G SALTED BUTTER, AT ROOM TEMPERATURE

2 TBSP COARSELY CHOPPED FRESH PARSLEY

2 TBSP COARSELY CHOPPED FRESH OREGANO

Soak the salt cod in the refrigerator for 2 to 3 days, changing the water once a day. Rinse one final time before cooking. Or, if you haven't planned ahead, soak the fish for 5 hours, rinse, and then break the fillets up into pieces. Soak again until you're ready to use it, changing the water frequently.

In a large frying pan over medium-low heat, cook the bacon for 10 minutes or until it has rendered some of its fat but is still soft and undercooked. Transfer the bacon to a paper towel-lined plate and set aside. Pour off most of the fat and set aside the still slightly greasy pan.

Preheat the oven to 350°F/180°C/gas 4. Pour the oil into a Dutch oven or large, deep, ovenproof frying pan. Add the potatoes, forming one overlapping layer. Put the fish fillets on top of the potatoes in a single layer. Layer the tomatoes, and then the sweet peppers and chile, on top of the fish. Finally, lay the bacon on top of it all, covering the vegetables as much as possible. Put the pot in the oven to bake, uncovered, for 40 minutes, or until the fish is fragrant and the potatoes are soft.

While the fish cooks, put the onion in the pan you cooked the bacon in with the leftover grease. Cook over low heat for 30 minutes or until the onion is soft and golden in color.

Toast the bread until crisp and spread generously with butter. Set the pieces of toast, cut in half if necessary, in shallow soup bowls. When the fish is done, cover the bacon with the onion and sprinkle the herbs over the top. Use a ladle or large spoon to portion the fish, vegetables, bacon, onions, and broth over the bread. You can now eat.

FISH NOTE:
There's no substitute for salt cod, but there are various grades. Most important, look for pure white, thick pieces. Norway, Iceland, and Spain still produce a great deal of salt cod; many swear by the quality of the Norwegian product. If you buy your salt cod from a reputable fish store, you'll likely end up with the good stuff. The best of the best is graded "superior extra." Look for superior grade or imperial. Salt cod is sometimes called *morue*, *bacalao*, or saltfish.

— TOSSED GREENS —

If you actually like the taste of salad greens—as opposed to
the heavy dressing that too often coats them—this one is for
you. It's all about the green, weedy mix just *barely* coated with
the best olive oil, salt, and a squeeze of lemon juice. The salad
should be dry—airy in the bowl. When you dress it, it should
not look any different other than showing a light shimmer
from that fine spritz of oil.

8 CUPS/340 G MIXED GREENS, INCLUDING ANY OF
THE FOLLOWING IN ANY COMBINATION: ARUGULA,
MÂCHE, BABY KALE, MIZUNA, BABY BEET GREENS,
ESCAROLE, RADICCHIO, TATSOI, SPINACH, FRISÉE,
AND BABY SWISS CHARD, RINSED AND DRIED

2 TBSP VERY GOOD EXTRA-VIRGIN OLIVE OIL

1 TBSP FRESH LEMON JUICE

FLAKY OR COARSE SALT

Put the clean, dry greens in a salad bowl. Just before you'll be
eating them, drizzle on the olive oil and toss until the oil coats
the leaves evenly. Squeeze on the lemon juice, add a pinch of salt,
and toss just a few times before serving.

BRAISED SABLEFISH
WITH PORK BELLY, LEEKS, FRENCH LENTILS, AND SHAVED FENNEL SALAD

SERVES 4

This is rustic French food with a kicker of pork belly. Add leeks, rich stock, thyme, and lentils with buttery sablefish. Serve with toast, either plain or Garlic (page 96) and lovely white wine from the Loire Valley. Consider a Sancerre that's just *slightly* out of your price range.

2 LB/910 G PORK BELLY

1 TBSP KOSHER SALT, PLUS ½ TSP

5 TBSP/70 G BUTTER

2 CUPS/350 G LEEKS, CUT INTO THIN ROUNDS

6 CUPS/960 ML CHICKEN OR FISH STOCK (PAGE 27)

3 SPRIGS FRESH THYME

1½ CUPS/330 G FRENCH PUY LENTILS

FOUR 4- TO 6-OZ/115- TO 170-G SABLEFISH FILLETS

2 TBSP CHAMPAGNE OR WHITE WINE VINEGAR

FLAKY OR COARSE SALT (OPTIONAL)

GARLIC TOAST (PAGE 96) OR PLAIN TOAST

Preheat the oven to 200°F/95°C. Place the pork belly in a large cast-iron pan and coat both sides with the 1 tbsp of kosher salt, positioning the belly skin-side up. Place the pan in the oven and cook, gently, for 5 hours.

When the belly is falling apart tender, place it on a cutting board and cut into 8 slices (they will be generous). Keep warm to be sure it's hot when it hits the plate.

Preheat the broiler to high, placing the rack in the middle of the oven or low enough to allow a large pot to fit. In a Dutch oven or a deep, ovenproof sauté pan set over medium heat, melt 3 tbsp of the butter and add the leeks. Cook, stirring frequently, for 5 to 8 minutes or until the leeks have softened. Remove the leeks from the pot and set aside. Add the stock, thyme, and lentils to the same pot. Cover and simmer over low heat for 20 to 25 minutes or until

the lentils are just tender. Remove from the heat, return the leeks
to the pot, and set the fish on the leeks and lentils, nestled in
the liquid. Broil for 6 to 10 minutes or until the fish shows brown
spots on the surface. Remove from the oven, transfer the fish to a
warm plate, and stir the remaining 2 tbsp of butter, the remaining
$1/2$ tsp of kosher salt, and the vinegar into the sauce. Taste for
salt and acidity, adding flaky or coarse salt and more vinegar as
needed. Ladle the liquid and leeks into bowls, put the fish on top,
the pork belly next to it, and a piece of Garlic Toast on the side.

FISH NOTE:
Often called black cod, this rich fish (another of its names is
butterfish) can be your substitute for Chilean sea bass. It's
just as delicious and sustainably fished in the United States,
Pacific, and Canada.

— SHAVED FENNEL SALAD —

A refreshing, crisp composition that will add a bright note
to the rich fish. The shaved white cheese contrasts with the
ruby pomegranate.

2 TO 3 FENNEL BULBS, TOUGH OUTER LAYER
REMOVED, TOPS TRIMMED, WITH A FEW
FRONDS RESERVED

1 TBSP OLIVE OIL

1 TBSP LEMON JUICE

PINCH OF FLAKY OR COARSE SALT

2 OZ/55 G PARMESAN CHEESE

1 CUP/50 G POMEGRANATE KERNELS
(OPTIONAL; IF IN SEASON)

Use your sharpest knife to cut the fennel into the thinnest rounds
possible. Lay the rounds on the cutting board and cut from top to
bottom to make thin lengths or spears. In a large serving bowl,
combine the fennel, olive oil, lemon juice, and salt and toss.
With a vegetable peeler, shave the Parmesan on top, and scatter
the pomegranate kernels over the Parmesan, if you're using them.
Finish with a few fennel fronds.

ORECCHIETTE WITH FLAKED PACIFIC HALIBUT, CHARRED ROMAINE, SWEET PEPPER, AND PINE NUTS

SERVES 4

This is an unusual pasta dish, which is a snap to put together. It gets its richness from the fish and a deep, smoky flavor from the charred romaine. The pepper adds a note of sweetness. Think weeknight meal with a friendly bottle of white or red wine. Yes, fish and red wine, especially in this case, is not a faux pas.

Warning: Avoid Chinese pine nuts. These can cause—at least in some people, and I'm one of them—pine nut syndrome, an unpleasant lingering bitter taste in your mouth that can last for days. Look for Italian or Turkish pine nuts—and buy from a reliable source.

KOSHER SALT

2 TO 3 HEADS ROMAINE LETTUCE

1 RED OR ORANGE BELL PEPPER, SEEDED AND QUARTERED

2 TBSP OLIVE OIL

8 OZ/225 G HALIBUT FILLET

1 LB/455 G ORECCHIETTE (ANY BITE-SIZE PASTA WILL WORK FINE)

2 TBSP VERY GOOD EXTRA-VIRGIN OLIVE OIL

FLAKY OR COARSE SALT AND BLACK PEPPER

1/4 CUP/10 G COARSELY CHOPPED FRESH BASIL

1/4 CUP/30 G ITALIAN PINE NUTS, TOASTED

PARMIGIANO-REGGIANO OR GRANA PADANO CHEESE, FRESHLY GRATED

Preheat your broiler to high and set the rack 3 to 5 in/7.5 to 12 cm from the heat source. Set a large pot of water to boil with 1 tsp of kosher salt added to it. To prepare the romaine, ruthlessly pull the outer leaves off the heads, leaving only the crispest, most perfect inner leaves. Rinse the heads, still intact, under cool water and then shake dry. Put the romaine and bell pepper in a large mixing bowl and toss with olive oil and 1/4 tsp of kosher salt.

Line a baking sheet with foil large enough for the romaine to fit in one layer. Crimp the edges up to catch the juice. Lay the romaine and pepper down on the foil. Run the fish around in any oil left behind in the bowl and place it on top of the romaine, skin-side up (if it has skin). Place the pan under the broiler and cook for 6 to 12 minutes until the fish is fragrant and has begun to yield its juices, or the lettuce is black in spots—really! Use a spatula to remove the fish before the lettuce if the lettuce isn't blackened but the fish is done. Remove from the oven and cut the romaine crosswise. Cut the pepper into bite-size pieces. Meanwhile, cook the pasta al dente, and reserve 1/4 cup/60 ml of the cooking water.

Toss the pasta with the reserved water along with the extra-virgin olive oil, romaine, peppers, and fish. Add a pinch of flaky or coarse salt and a generous grind of black pepper, taste, and adjust for salt. Portion out into pasta bowls, finishing each serving with the basil, pine nuts, and Parmigiano.

FISH NOTE:
Pacific Halibut is in relatively good supply, but any flaky fish will be delicious here: Atlantic haddock from Canada, Norway, or Russia, or Pacific cod, Arctic char, coho salmon, or even a handful of sardines.

ALMOND-CRUSTED PACIFIC HADDOCK
WITH FENNEL CARROTS AND RICED CHIVE POTATOES

SERVES 4

Grinding a few almonds to use as a coating for your haddock takes
minutes. Their nutty richness, toasted as your fish cooks in brown
butter, is worth slowing down for. This kind of elemental meal
calls for a terrific French white wine, perhaps a flinty Premier
Crū Chablis from Burgundy. Throw together a simple green salad
(Tossed Greens, page 77) for after your meal, and maybe a hunk
of exotically stinky French cheese.

1 CUP/140 G WHOLE RAW ALMONDS	LEAVES OF 2 FRESH THYME SPRIGS (ABOUT 1 TBSP)
½ TSP KOSHER SALT	1 LEMON, QUARTERED
¼ CUP/30 G ALL-PURPOSE FLOUR	FLAKY OR COARSE SALT
1½ LB/680 G HADDOCK FILLETS	FENNEL CARROTS (RECIPE FOLLOWS)
2 TO 4 TBSP/30 TO 55 G BUTTER	RICED CHIVE POTATOES (RECIPE FOLLOWS)

Preheat the oven to 175°F/80°C. In the bowl of a food processor,
combine the almonds, kosher salt, and flour. Pulse with the blade
until there are no large chunks of nut. The mixture should be
coarse, not chunky. Put the nut mixture in a shallow bowl and dip
the fish in it, thoroughly coating both sides. Put 1 or 2 tbsp of the
butter in a large, heavy frying pan over high heat. When the butter
is hot and just beginning to brown, lay some of the fish in the pan
in a single layer. Cook for 2 to 3 minutes per side or until the nut
coating is a deep, crispy brown. Transfer the fish to individual

plates and place in the warming oven. Scrape the browned bits from the pan, add more butter, and repeat until all the fish is cooked. Add some of the Fennel Carrots and Riced Chive Potatoes to each plate. Finish by sprinkling the whole plate—potatoes and all—with thyme leaves. Give the fish a good squeeze of lemon juice, leaving the wedge for each diner to finish off, and bring the plates to the table hot.

FISH NOTE:
Pacific haddock is in relatively good supply, but any flaky fish will be delicious here: Pacific halibut, Atlantic or Pacific cod, Arctic char, coho salmon, or even a handful of sardines.

— FENNEL CARROTS —

Pretty, elegant, and subtle. I love this very French combination done the way Louis Diat made his carrots—in a pan with a splash of water and plenty of butter.

1 LARGE FENNEL BULB, TOUGH OUTER LAYER REMOVED, THINLY SLICED

8 TO 10 MEDIUM CARROTS, PEELED AND CUT INTO MATCHSTICKS

LEAVES OF 2 FRESH THYME SPRIGS (ABOUT 1 TBSP)

1 TBSP FENNEL SEEDS

1 TBSP WATER

2 TBSP BUTTER

½ TSP KOSHER SALT

FLAKY OR COARSE SALT

In a large pot with a tight-fitting lid, combine the fennel, carrots, thyme, fennel seeds, water, butter, and kosher salt. Cover, place over high heat, and cook for 8 to 10 minutes, shaking the pan frequently. The carrots should caramelize slightly, showing a little color on the edges. The fennel should be tender but not mushy. Give the mixture a final pinch of flaky or coarse salt before serving.

— RICED CHIVE POTATOES —

If you aspire to be a superhero of the potato world, try ricing
your potatoes instead of mashing them. You'll never make them
any other way again. The light, airy results will stun you.
Chives add flavor and color. Ricers are easy to find—you can
spend $100 on a really nice French model, or you can probably
find one at an antiques store or on eBay for next to nothing.
Buy one big enough to fit at least three potatoes.

2 LB/910 G YUKON GOLD OR OTHER YELLOW-
FLESHED POTATOES

1 CUP/240 ML HEAVY CREAM

3 TBSP BUTTER

BLACK PEPPER

1 TSP KOSHER SALT

¼ CUP/10 G THIN ROUNDS OF SNIPPED FRESH
CHIVES

Peel the potatoes and, as you work, place them in a large pot
filled two-thirds of the way with cold water. Be sure the
potatoes are covered with water, bring to a boil, and cook for
20 to 25 minutes or until a knife inserted into the center of
a potato meets no resistance.

While the potatoes cook, heat the cream, butter, pepper, and salt
in a small saucepan. Do not let the mixture boil but do let it
get very hot. Be sure the butter is melted. Look for a light bubbling in the cream, indicating a near boil. Set aside.

Pour the potatoes into a colander to drain them, and then force
them through the ricer, back into the pot you cooked them in. Do
not stir, tempting as it will be. When you're almost ready to sit
down and eat, pour the hot cream and butter mixture over the
potatoes, add the chives, and stir *just* enough to incorporate.
Taste, adding additional salt if needed. Ah, the joys of the cow
and the tuber!

ALASKAN SALMON
WITH BÉARNAISE, ROASTED CIPOLLINI ONIONS AND NEW POTATOES, AND PARMESAN-ARUGULA SALAD

SERVES 4

Béarnaise is the epitome of French sauces and just one of the many reasons to love classic French cuisine. Paired with fresh wild Alaskan salmon and served for your Monday meal, it will give you the strength to get through any week. If you don't have any stock, poach the fish in a mixture of white wine (not superoaked Chardonnay) and water. Add a few herbs, like thyme, bay leaves, and parsley, to the liquid.

4 LARGE, LEAFY SPRIGS FRESH TARRAGON

2/3 CUP/165 ML DRY WHITE WINE

3 TBSP WHITE WINE OR CHAMPAGNE VINEGAR

3 TBSP CHOPPED SHALLOTS

3 EGG YOLKS

1 CUP/225 G UNSALTED BUTTER, AT ROOM TEMPERATURE, CUT INTO 8 CHUNKS

1/2 TSP KOSHER SALT

5 TO 6 CUPS/1.2 TO 1.4 L CHICKEN, FISH (PAGE 27), OR VEGETABLE STOCK, OR A MIXTURE OF WHITE WINE AND WATER WITH HERBS

FOUR 4- TO 6-OZ/115- TO 170-G SALMON FILLETS

To make the sauce, in a small frying pan set over medium heat, combine 2 sprigs of the tarragon with the white wine, vinegar, and shallots. Simmer for 5 to 8 minutes or until the liquid has reduced by about two-thirds. Remove the tarragon sprigs and transfer the remaining liquid to the top of a double boiler set over medium-low heat. Improvise if you don't have one by setting a metal or heat-proof ceramic bowl over a pot; just be sure the water on the bottom

of your double boiler is barely simmering and is not touching the bowl you're working in. Before the reduction liquid begins to heat up again too much, whisk in the egg yolks, one at time. Heat the mixture in the double boiler for 2 to 3 minutes or until it's quite hot and has thickened to the consistency of heavy cream. Add the butter, one chunk at a time, whisking all the while. When all the butter has been added, turn off the heat and remove the top of the double boiler from the bottom. Stem and then chop the remaining 2 sprigs of tarragon. Whisk them into the mixture along with the salt.

To cook the fish, pour the stock into a large, deep sauté pan and set over medium heat. Bring the stock just to a simmer and gently place the fish in the hot liquid. It should be almost submerged, depending on how thick the fillets are. Cover and cook at just a simmer for 6 to 8 minutes before checking for doneness. The center of the salmon should be dark orange, not light coral, and still translucent. A paring knife should go into its center without resistance, however. Gently transfer the fish to warm plates and just before serving, spoon the béarnaise over the top of the fish. Bring any leftover sauce to the table.

FISH NOTE:
Look for wild Alaskan salmon or farmed coho salmon or Arctic char.
Avoid: farmed Atlantic salmon.

— ROASTED CIPOLLINI ONIONS —
AND NEW POTATOES

Simple and fast, this is the dreamiest of side dishes if you're
looking for a vehicle for that béarnaise.

1 LB/455 G NEW POTATOES

1 LB/455 G CIPOLLINI ONIONS, BLANCHED
AND PEELED

2 TBSP OLIVE OIL

½ TSP KOSHER SALT

Preheat the oven to 500°F/260°C/gas 10. Fill a large saucepan with
cold water, add the potatoes, and place over high heat. Once the
water comes to a boil, lower the heat to keep the water at a steady
simmer and cook the potatoes for 15 to 20 minutes or until they
are tender but not falling apart. Test a potato by inserting a
paring knife. There should be little resistance. Drain and place
in a large mixing bowl. Add the onions, olive oil, and salt and
toss. Spread out on a baking sheet (parchment-lined, if you like),
and roast for 12 to 15 minutes or until the edges of the onions and
potatoes begin to brown. Don't be hasty and take them out before
they show some color.

— PARMESAN-ARUGULA SALAD —

If you haven't guessed as much already, I have a thing for
arugula. This is just an excuse to eat it, mixed in with shavings
of umami-inducing Parmesan.

5 OZ/140 G ARUGULA

1 TBSP VERY GOOD EXTRA-VIRGIN OLIVE OIL

1 TSP FRESH LEMON JUICE

FLAKY OR COARSE SALT

¼ CUP/30 G FRESHLY GRATED PARMESAN CHEESE

Just before you're ready to eat, in a large serving bowl, toss
together the arugula, olive oil, lemon juice, and a tiny pinch of
salt—remember, the Parmesan is salty. The arugula should not be
weighed down—instead, it still should be light and airy, with a
fine glisten of oil. Scatter the Parmesan over the top and bring
it to the table.

GRILLED YELLOWFIN TUNA
WITH MUSTARD AÏOLI, DOMINO POTATOES, AND BLACKENED TOMATOES

SERVES 4

It's a summery July day, there's freshly mowed lawn, and the flowers are in bloom: I recommend taking this meal outdoors. Grilled tuna with mustard-scented garlic mayo, crispy potatoes, and just-ripe tomatoes are worth a leisurely meal in the back-yard. Let the food cool a bit—there's no hurry, and it might taste even better. Put some French rosé under ice in a metal tub and get out the cloth napkins. Think of it as a grown-up picnic. Keep in mind that the tuna goes on and comes off the grill in a flash. Cook your tomatoes first. The Domino Potatoes take a little time, too. Keep the rosé coming.

FOUR 4- TO 6-OZ/115- TO 170-G YELLOWFIN TUNA STEAKS

OLIVE OIL FOR THE FISH

FLAKY OR COARSE SALT AND BLACK PEPPER

¼ CUP/10 G MIXED FRESH THYME, BASIL, PARSLEY, AND OREGANO LEAVES

MUSTARD AÏOLI (RECIPE FOLLOWS)

DOMINO POTATOES (RECIPE FOLLOWS)

BLACKENED TOMATOES (RECIPE FOLLOWS)

Build a hot fire in a charcoal or wood grill or preheat a gas grill to high.

Preheat the oven to 175°F/80°C. Rub the fish all over with a little olive oil. Cook for 3 minutes on the first side before carefully turning the fish and cooking for another 2 to 3 minutes on the second side. How long the fish takes to cook all depends on the thickness of the fish and how hot your grill is. Fresh, beautiful tuna steaks should be quite rare at the center; overcooked fish will be dry and gray. The fish should be about 125°F/52°C at the center—the same temperature as a rare steak. Err on the side of undercooking and transfer the fish to the warming oven before you plate it. This will bring a little heat to the center.

Build each plate with a few fanned-out Domino Potatoes, the fish, and a tomato, blackened-side up. Drizzle a generous portion of the sauce over the fish, scatter with fresh herbs, and bring them to the table.

FISH NOTE:
Buy troll- or pole-caught yellowfin tuna from U.S. waters. Never buy bluefin, ranched or wild. Substitute mahi mahi or any whole fish with its scales left on and coated with plenty of coarse salt to prevent sticking.

— MUSTARD AÏOLI —

Mayonnaise is practically a food group for my southern friends. Made fresh and goosed up with a little acidity, garlic, and enough mustard to give it a ping, this version will take you through any meal.

2 EGG YOLKS

2 TBSP FRESH LEMON JUICE

1 CUP/240 ML LIGHT OLIVE OIL (NOT EXTRA-VIRGIN)

½ HEAD GARLIC, CLOVES PEELED AND MINCED

2 TBSP LOW-ACID, GRAINY MUSTARD SUCH AS MAILLE OLD STYLE

½ TSP KOSHER SALT

BLACK PEPPER

In a large metal bowl, beat the egg yolks vigorously using a balloon whisk. After the yolks turn light yellow, whisk in the lemon juice. Drizzle a tiny bit of olive oil into the mixture, whisking all the while. Continue adding the olive oil in a thin stream, whisking constantly, until it's all incorporated. The mixture will stiffen as the oil forms an emulsion with the egg yolks.

Add the garlic, mustard, salt, and some pepper. Mix well and transfer to a pretty bowl. Refrigerate for 30 minutes before serving to give it body.

— DOMINO POTATOES —

Cutting these potatoes into rectangles is worth the trouble; it's a treat to have such a stunning potato dish to bring to the table.

5 RUSSET POTATOES, PEELED AND SET IN A BOWL OF COLD WATER

4 TBSP/55 G BUTTER, MELTED

½ TSP KOSHER SALT

Preheat the oven to 400°F/200°C/gas 6. Cut the potatoes into rectangles by cutting off the rounded parts on each of the four sides and on each end. Beginning at one end, cut each potato into thin slices—but not so thin that the slice doesn't hold its shape. Put the slices in a bowl and toss gently with the butter and salt. Lay the potatoes in four rows in a 12-by-9-in/30.5-by-23-cm baking dish. Each row should look almost like toppled dominoes (if the dominoes were a little irregular and more square than rectangular). The four rows of potatoes should fit with just a little space between them. Bake for 40 to 50 minutes or until the edges are toasty brown—even black in spots—and the potatoes feel soft when a knife is inserted in the center.

— BLACKENED TOMATOES —

Look for good quality tomatoes. As a rule, heirloom varieties have the best flavor and texture. Just be sure the tomatoes you use are fairly firm. Overripe ones will disintegrate on the hot grill like cotton candy in the rain.

2 TOMATOES, HALVED ON THE EQUATOR

OLIVE OIL FOR RUBBING ON THE TOMATOES

FLAKY OR COARSE SALT

Rub the cut side of each tomato half with a little oil and lay them on the hottest part of the fire, cut-side down. Leave them, letting them cook there until they begin to shrink slightly around the edges, 10 to 15 minutes. Use a spatula to take them off the fire before they disintegrate. The faces should be blackened. Give each one a good pinch of salt before serving.

ARCTIC CHAR
WITH TARRAGON VINAIGRETTE, ROASTED SUNCHOKES, RADICCHIO, AND CARROTS

SERVES 4

Arctic char, with its crispy, irresistible skin, paired with this pretty mix of vegetables, makes quite a lovely plate. The tarragon vinaigrette mixes with every flavor, adding brightness and the grassy, anise flavor of the herb. A crispy, sour baguette smeared with sweet butter would round out the meal.

---

1 TSP KOSHER SALT

FOUR 6-OZ/170-G ARCTIC CHAR FILLETS, DEBONED
(SEE A NOTE ABOUT FISH BONES, PAGE 26)

4 TBSP/55 G BUTTER, CUT INTO 8 BITS

1/4 CUP/60 ML OLIVE OIL

2 TBSP WHITE WINE VINEGAR

2 TBSP DIJON MUSTARD

2 TBSP MINCED SHALLOT

BLACK PEPPER

2 TBSP CHOPPED FRESH TARRAGON

FLAKY OR COARSE SALT

Preheat the broiler to high. Place a rack 3 to 5 in/7.5 to 12 cm from the heat source. Line a baking sheet or large ovenproof frying pan with foil, crimping the sides all around so that any juices released from the fish will be captured. Sprinkle 1/2 tsp of the kosher salt on the nonskin side of the fish fillets. Place the fish on the foil skin-side up with a bit of butter under each fillet. Dab another bit on the skin. Cook the fish for 6 to 10 minutes. The cooking time varies widely, depending on the strength of your broiler and the thickness of the fish. Arctic char, like salmon, should be served just cooked or still translucent at its center. When the skin shows little blackened flecks here and there, it's certainly done—it's also delicious that way.

To make the vinaigrette, in a small bowl mix together the remaining 1/2 tsp of kosher salt, the olive oil, vinegar, mustard, shallot, pepper, and tarragon.

Serve by spooning a pool of the vinaigrette in the center of each plate. Place the fish on top and surround it with the sunchokes, radicchio, and carrots. Sprinkle with a pinch of flaky or coarse salt.

FISH NOTE:
Substitute wild Alaskan salmon or coho salmon for the Arctic char. Avoid: farmed Atlantic salmon.

— ROASTED SUNCHOKES, — RADICCHIO, AND CARROTS

Many people eat sunchokes raw. I do, too, but I also love them cut into meaty rounds, tossed with olive oil, and roasted until they're soft on the outside and crispy at the center. Adding carrots and radicchio only makes this simple root shine. Look for baby carrots at the farmers' market or for those at the grocery store with the tops still on—they're much fresher. Remove the tops as soon as you get home. The radicchio adds bite to this pretty fall vegetable mix.

1 LB/455 G SUNCHOKES, WELL SCRUBBED AND CUT INTO 1-IN-/2.5-CM-THICK ROUNDS

1 SMALL HEAD RADICCHIO, CUT INTO RIBBONS

4 CARROTS OR 8 BABY CARROTS, PEELED AND CUT INTO 1/2-IN/12-MM ROUNDS

1 TBSP OLIVE OIL

1/2 TSP KOSHER SALT

3 CHIVES, SNIPPED INTO THIN ROUNDS

FLAKY OR COARSE SALT

Preheat the oven to 500°F/260°C/gas 10. In a large mixing bowl, toss the sunchokes, radicchio, and carrots with the olive oil and kosher salt. Spread the vegetables out on a baking sheet (parchment-lined, if you like) and roast for 8 to 12 minutes or until the carrots and sunchokes show a little brown on the edges. Toss with the chives and finish with a pinch of flaky or coarse salt.

MUSSELS
WITH CREAM, SAFFRON, AND ANGEL HAIR, GARLIC TOAST, AND GRAPEFRUIT-FENNEL SALAD

SERVES 4

The flavor of these plump bivalves is brilliant when gently paired with butter, cream, and spices. Saffron and mussels are as natural together as oysters and Champagne. Add a little cream, a bit of crispy fennel, and some delicate pasta, and you have a luxurious yet uncomplicated meal.

3 LB/1.4 KG MUSSELS, CLEANED AND DEBEARDED, IF NECESSARY

1 CUP/240 ML WHITE WINE

2 GARLIC CLOVES, THINLY SLICED

1 SMALL SHALLOT, CHOPPED

6 STRIPS LEMON ZEST, JULIENNED

6 SPRIGS FRESH THYME

1 LB/455 G ANGEL-HAIR PASTA, COOKED IN BOILING SALTED WATER UNTIL AL DENTE

3 TBSP BUTTER

1 FENNEL BULB, TOUGH OUTER LAYER REMOVED, SLIVERED, WITH FENNEL FRONDS RESERVED

1 CUP/240 ML HEAVY CREAM

1 TO 2 TSP SAFFRON, LIGHTLY CRUSHED

1/4 CUP/10 G CHOPPED FRESH PARSLEY

FLAKY OR COARSE SALT AND BLACK PEPPER

In a large Dutch oven or pot with a lid, combine the mussels, white wine, garlic, shallot, lemon zest, and thyme and set over high heat for 10 minutes or until all the mussels are open. (Discard any that have not opened.) Turn off the heat and use tongs or a slotted spoon to transfer the mussels to a mixing bowl. Reserve the cooking liquid in the pot. Once the mussels are cool enough to handle, remove the meat from the shells and set aside. (Discard the shells.)

Once the pasta has cooked, toss it with the butter. Set aside.

Return the cooking liquid from the mussels to medium heat and reduce for 5 minutes, or until about 1½ cups/360 ml of liquid remain. Add the fennel bulb, cream, and saffron and reduce for 2 to 3 minutes over high heat. Just before serving, add the parsley and return the mussels to the sauce to reheat. Line four pasta bowls with pasta and portion out the sauce and mussels over the top. Finish with the fennel fronds, lightly torn, a pinch of flaky or coarse salt, and a generous grind of black pepper.

— GARLIC TOAST —

My husband and I go out to breakfast together pretty often. We go to the Frenchtown Cafe, the cutest, best little diner in town, and we order the same thing every time: poached eggs on rye toast. One morning, toast that was perfectly browned and buttered arrived on my plate. All I could say was, "Whoever made this must have a PhD in toast." There are worse things to have a doctorate in. (Trust me, I know.) Treat your toast with the respect it deserves. I consider properly made toast a highly evolved, underrated food, with or without garlic.

1 HEAD GARLIC, CLOVES PEELED AND LIGHTLY CRUSHED

¼ CUP/60 ML OLIVE OIL

5 LARGE CHIVES, CHOPPED

¼ TSP KOSHER SALT

2 TBSP BUTTER

4 LARGE SLICES LEVAIN OR ANY FLAVORFUL, CHEWY SOURDOUGH BREAD

FLAKY OR COARSE SALT

In a blender, small food processor, or mortar combine the garlic, oil, chives, and kosher salt. Work until the garlic is no longer in visible chunks. Transfer to a small saucepan, add the butter, and place over very low heat until the butter melts and the mixture begins to simmer. Cook for 8 to 10 minutes. The butter should not brown.

Toast the bread until crisp and lightly browned. Paint on or gently drizzle the fat onto the hot bread. Be sure it's adequately salted and that you have plenty at hand!

— GRAPEFRUIT-FENNEL SALAD —

Lettuce in salad has its place, but a salad without lettuce sheds
its own boundaries to become a dish in itself. This lettuce-free
winter salad is one I make often: crisp, freshly toasted almond
slivers with pink grapefruit and crunchy fennel. Use high-end
olive oil and a Meyer lemon, if you can find one.

1 LARGE FENNEL BULB, TOUGH OUTER LAYER
REMOVED, CUT INTO THIN ROUNDS

3 PINK GRAPEFRUIT, PEELED

3/4 CUP/100 G SLIVERED ALMONDS, TOASTED
(SEE PAGE 30)

2 TBSP VERY GOOD EXTRA-VIRGIN OLIVE OIL

1 TBSP FRESH LEMON JUICE

1/2 TSP KOSHER SALT

Stack the fennel rounds and cut across them to make bite-size
chunks. Section the grapefruit, using your hands to get rid of as
much of the membrane as possible, and cut into chunks. Toss the
fennel, grapefruit, and 1/2 cup/60 g of the almonds together in a
salad or large mixing bowl. Add the olive oil, lemon juice, and salt.
Toss thoroughly. Finish by sprinkling the remaining slivered
almonds on top.

SCALLOP-CHORIZO SPAGHETTI
WITH FENNEL—CRACKER BREAD SALAD

SERVES 4

The best thing about this recipe is the way the spicy oil from the chorizo turns the spaghetti a glistening orange. Try chopping the pasta or breaking it up before you boil the noodles. It gives the dish a rustic look. Fuss free, fast, pork-flavored, and made with sustainable scallops. How good can it get?

2 TBSP OLIVE OIL

8 OZ/225 G SPANISH CHORIZO, CUT INTO 1/4-IN/6-MM SLICES

2 GARLIC CLOVES, MINCED

1 LB/455 G SPAGHETTI, COOKED AL DENTE

2 TBSP VERY GOOD EXTRA-VIRGIN OLIVE OIL

KOSHER SALT AND BLACK PEPPER

12 OZ/340 G SCALLOPS

1/4 CUP/10 G CHOPPED FRESH PARSLEY

Put the olive oil in a frying pan set over medium heat, add the chorizo in one layer, and cook for 10 to 15 minutes, turning at the midway point, until the pieces are well browned and crispy on the edges—you might even see some black spots. Transfer the chorizo to a plate, leaving behind the oil. Add the garlic to the pan and cook gently for 1 to 2 minutes until soft but not browned. Pour the oil from the pan and the garlic into a small bowl and set aside, leaving behind a slick of oil for cooking the scallops. Once the pasta has cooked, toss it in a large bowl with the extra-virgin olive oil and the garlic and oil from the chorizo. Add salt and black pepper until it's perfectly seasoned.

Place the oily chorizo pan over high heat until it's very hot. Put the scallops in the pan and cook for 2 to 3 minutes or until well seared on just one side. Flip them and cook for 20 seconds before transferring to a plate. Portion out the pasta in bowls, with some of the chorizo and scallops, seared-side up, on each. Sprinkle the parsley on top and serve.

FISH NOTE:
Both bay and sea scallops are relatively abundant and widely farmed. They should appear moist and plump and smell of nothing but the sea.

— FENNEL–CRACKER BREAD SALAD —

I love salads, almost all salads, but this one sneaks in all of my favorite ingredients—fennel, feta, cherry tomatoes, herbs. Add the radishes and cracker bread and it's bliss.

1 FENNEL BULB, TOUGH OUTER LAYER REMOVED,
CUT INTO THIN ROUNDS

3½ OZ/100 G SHEEP'S MILK FETA, CRUMBLED

5 PIECES SEEDED CRACKER BREAD,
CRUMBLED INTO BITE-SIZE PIECES

1 PT/340 G CHERRY TOMATOES,
PREFERABLY SUN GOLD

5 FRENCH BREAKFAST RADISHES, TRIMMED AND
CUT INTO ROUNDS

LEAVES OF 2 FRESH THYME SPRIGS

5 FRESH BASIL LEAVES, ROLLED AND CUT
INTO RIBBONS

2 TBSP VERY GOOD EXTRA-VIRGIN OLIVE OIL

SQUEEZE OF FRESH LEMON JUICE

FLAKY OR COARSE SALT AND BLACK PEPPER

Combine the fennel, feta, cracker bread, tomatoes, radishes, thyme, and basil together in a salad bowl. Just before serving, drizzle on the olive oil and toss thoroughly. Add a good-size squeeze of lemon juice, a pinch of salt, and some black pepper. Toss again and taste for salt and acidity.

ROCK SHRIMP AND FAVA BEAN RISOTTO
WITH LARDON-ENDIVE SALAD

SERVES 4

Cooking risotto is famously tricky. The rice can't be mushy and shapeless; nor can it be crunchy and stiff. As with almost every-thing else in life, timing is everything: the best strategy is to pay attention when it matters most. That does not mean you should chain yourself to your pot, nervously tending to each minor alteration of texture. The risotto will cook beautifully if you stand guard at the end, as it transitions from al dente to mushy. (It will do this in the time it takes to rinse the tasting spoon.) If you do mess it up, relax. The sweet rock shrimp, bright fava beans, and rich dairy are your guarantee it'll be sublime anyway.

3 1/2 CUPS/840 ML SHRIMP, CHICKEN, OR FISH STOCK (PAGE 27)

2 TBSP OLIVE OIL

2 SHALLOTS, MINCED

1 CUP/215 G ARBORIO RICE

1 LARGE GARLIC CLOVE, CHOPPED

GRATED ZEST AND JUICE OF 1 LEMON (PREFERABLY ORGANIC)

1/3 CUP/45 G FRESHLY GRATED PARMIGIANO-REGGIANO CHEESE, PLUS MORE TO FINISH THE PLATES

KOSHER SALT

3 TBSP BUTTER

1 1/3 CUPS/285 G FRESH FAVA BEANS, BLANCHED AND REMOVED FROM THEIR OUTER CASING (SUBSTITUTE FRESH OR FROZEN LIMA BEANS OR EDAMAME)

FLAKY OR COARSE SALT

1 1/2 LB/680 G ROCK SHRIMP

1/4 CUP/60 ML FINO SHERRY

1/2 TSP CHILE FLAKES, LIGHTLY CRUSHED

BLACK PEPPER

1/4 CUP/10 G FRESH BASIL LEAVES, ROLLED AND CUT INTO THREADS

Bring the stock to a boil in a large saucepan. Transfer the hot stock to a heat-proof container and set aside. In the same sauce-pan over medium heat, combine the olive oil and shallots. Cook the

⇒

shallots for 2 to 3 minutes or until just soft. Add the rice and cook for another 2 to 3 minutes or until the rice is well coated and heated in the oil. Add the garlic and half the lemon zest. Cook for another 1 or 2 minutes or until the garlic is just fragrant, but not colored. Add 2 cups/480 ml of stock, stir, and turn the heat to medium-low. Cook, stirring frequently to prevent sticking, for 10 to 15 minutes or until the stock is mostly absorbed, before adding more stock in 1/2-cup/120-ml increments. After about 20 minutes, you'll notice the rice has increased in volume and gained a thick, creamy consistency. It's almost done. Lower the heat to slow the cooking and taste the rice. It should be smooth and creamy, with a lovely body of texture, but no actual crunch. If it's done, turn off the heat and stir in the remaining half of the lemon zest, 1 tbsp of the lemon juice, and the Parmigiano. Taste for salt, lemon flavor, and acidity, adding a pinch or two of kosher salt or a little more lemon juice, as you like.

In a large sauté pan, melt 1 tbsp of the butter over high heat. Add the fava beans and cook for 2 to 3 minutes or until they're hot and have lost their raw edge. Give them a pinch of flaky or coarse salt, transfer to a plate, and set aside. Lower the heat to medium, and melt the remaining 2 tbsp of butter. Add the shrimp, Sherry, and chile flakes and cook for 3 to 5 minutes, stirring frequently, until the shrimp are *just* cooked. (If you're not using rock shrimp, you'll need to cook the shrimp longer.) Sprinkle with the leftover lemon juice, a little flaky or coarse salt, and good grind of black pepper.

In shallow bowls or on dinner plates, portion out the risotto with the shrimp and beans. Finish with a scattering of basil and freshly grated Parmigiano.

FISH NOTE:
Rock shrimp are a species of shrimp. They are smaller and their shells are soft, so they do not need to be peeled. When it comes to shrimp, wild-caught and farmed from the United States or European Union are the best choices, with wild spot prawns from Alaska and wild pink shrimp from Oregon being the best of the best. Avoid: farm-raised shrimp from Asia, including those from China, India, Thailand, and Malaysia.

— LARDON-ENDIVE SALAD —

This classic salad is not the prettiest you'll ever see, but what it lacks in looks it makes up for in taste.

8 OZ/225 G BACON, CUT INTO SQUARES

1 SHALLOT, CHOPPED

1 TBSP BALSAMIC OR RED WINE VINEGAR

2 TBSP OLIVE OIL

¼ TSP KOSHER SALT

BLACK PEPPER

3 HEADS ENDIVE LETTUCE, CUT INTO COARSE ROUNDS

2 EGGS, SEMISOFT-BOILED FOR 7 MINUTES

FLAKY OR COARSE SALT (OPTIONAL)

Cook the bacon in a medium skillet over medium heat until crisp. Pour off the excess fat, without scraping the pan. Return the pan to the heat and add the shallot. Sauté the shallot until just soft, 2 minutes or so. Remove the pan from the heat and add the vinegar, olive oil, kosher salt, and a good grind of black pepper. Scrape the dressing from the pan into a small bowl. Put the endive and lardons in a serving bowl.

Just before serving, toss the salad with the dressing, using only what you think you need to coat the lettuce. Whack the top off the eggs with a knife, and use a teaspoon to scoop the eggs on top of the salad. The yolks, which should be soft or even a bit runny, are part of the dressing, too. Add flaky or coarse salt and plenty of black pepper and toss.

CHAPTER 3

LATIN FISH

LATIN FISH

Bright, spicy, and bold is how I would define the food in this chapter. Get in the spirit of sitting around, sharing a big, informal feast. There are lots and lots of chiles—get ready for some heat. Remember—fat, not ice, is the best antidote for overindulgence. That means *crema*, guacamole, or even a slightly greasy tortilla chip.

Be sure to have lots of well-cleaned cilantro on hand. It can be gritty; float it in a big bowl of cold water to thoroughly clean it, and then dry it carefully. Nobody likes grit! *Crema* and sour cream are fairly interchangeable. I like *crema* because it tends to be a little more sour and liquid than sour cream. I call for serranos and jalapeños for the most part—they're the most widely available chiles out there. Just be aware that each chile varies greatly in how much heat it delivers. As for spices, be sure to have a fresh jar of cumin seeds, some whole coriander, and a way to grind them as you use them. It makes a big difference to work with fresh spices!

DRINKS

Drinking is easy—beer, lime, and tequila, not necessarily in that order. Don't cheat when you mix up your margaritas: fresh lime juice, the best triple sec (go easy), and top-shelf tequila. If you prefer something to cool down with that is nonalcoholic, make a pitcher of limeade with fresh lime juice and agave nectar. (You could even add tequila to that, should you wish.)

AT THE TABLE

I like my table set with bright, supersaturated Southwestern colors. It makes for a festive look with dishes of diced avocado, chopped chiles, quartered limes, minced onions, and extra *crema*. Making a jar of Smoky Sweet Hot Sauce (page 211) will save you from the indignities of inferior jarred hot sauce. Don't forget a kitchen towel full of warm tortillas—or a bowl of handmade chips.

SWEETS

One of the greatest pleasures after indulging in spicy food is the contrast of ice. This might come in the form of a lime-tequila sorbet or perhaps in the creamier form of a dulce de leche ice cream. I like to sprinkle mine with a pinch of flaky salt or serve it with a slightly salty nut cookie on the side.

WHOLE ROASTED BARRAMUNDI,
HEARTS OF PALM WITH CAIPIRINHA DRESSING, FAROFA, ORANGE SEGMENTS, AND BLACK BEANS

SERVES 4

I've got a friend who's a brilliant, intuitive cook and grew up in Brazil. This meal is inspired by his food and festive spirit. The caipirinha dressing is uncannily good with the hearts of palm—if you don't drink it first. Instead, make yourself a caipirinha cocktail to go with the meal—it would be a shame to waste all that cachaça.

TWO 1-LB/455-G WHOLE BARRAMUNDI, GUTTED AND SCALED, HEADS LEFT ON

1/2 CUP/125 G KOSHER SALT

BLACK BEANS (PAGE 132)

HEARTS OF PALM WITH CAIPIRINHA DRESSING (RECIPE FOLLOWS)

2 NAVEL ORANGES, PEELED AND CUT INTO MEMBRANE-FREE BITE-SIZE CHUNKS

FAROFA (OPTIONAL; RECIPE FOLLOWS)

1/4 CUP/10 G CHOPPED FRESH PARSLEY

FLAKY OR COARSE SALT

Clean and oil the grates of your grill thoroughly. Build a medium fire in a charcoal or wood grill or preheat a gas grill to medium.

Set the fish on a plate. After salting the interior of each fish with a pinch of the kosher salt, coat the outside of the fish with the remaining kosher salt to form a light crust.

Place the fish on the hottest part of the grill for 6 to 8 minutes. Carefully turn the fish and cook the other side for 6 to 8 minutes. Don't worry if the skin is blackened or dark in spots. The fish is done when the interior temperature is 135°F/57°C, or when both sides of the fish are flaky and forgiving when a knife is inserted. Transfer the fish to a platter.

To serve, remove the top fillet of a fish—which is one portion—and then grab the head and remove the skeleton right to the tail. Take off the skin and salt. The bottom fillet should be intact and ready to serve. Repeat with the other fish. Serve with the Black Beans, Hearts of Palm with Caipirinha Dressing, orange segments, and the Farofa sprinkled on top, if making. Finish the plate with the parsley scattered over everything and a pinch of flaky or coarse salt. (For more on serving whole fish, see page 23.)

<u>FISH NOTE:</u>
Look for barramundi that were farmed in fully recirculating systems, which is done in the United States and in Australia. Avoid: wild barramundi, as it is overfished. Substitute other whole fish such as branzino (farmed) or black or striped bass (farmed or wild-caught).

— HEARTS OF PALM — WITH CAIPIRINHA DRESSING

As noted, try not to drink this dressing—or serve it to small children. It's high in alcohol.

¼ CUP/60 ML CACHAÇA

JUICE OF 1 LIME

¼ CUP/60 ML OLIVE OIL

1 TBSP SUPERFINE SUGAR

TWO 14-OZ/400-G CANS HEARTS OF PALM OR PALMITOS, RINSED, DRAINED, AND CUT INTO 1-IN-/2.5-CM-THICK ROUNDS

2 TOMATOES, PREFERABLY HEIRLOOM, CUT INTO BITE-SIZE CHUNKS

FLAKY OR COARSE SALT

In the bottom of a serving bowl, whisk together the cachaça, lime juice, olive oil, and sugar. Add the hearts of palm and tomatoes and toss. Finish with a tiny pinch of salt just before serving.

— FAROFA —

Farofa is painfully difficult to find. Don't worry if you have to skip it. That said, it lends a kind of delicious starchy quality to everything on your plate that's pretty great. Look for it, and buy it when you see it!

1 CUP/110 G FAROFA OR MANIOC FLOUR

Preheat the oven to 300°F/150°C/gas 2. Spread out the farofa on a baking sheet and toast for 10 to 12 minutes or until it smells toasty.

YELLOWFIN TUNA SLIDERS
WITH CHIPOTLE MAYONNAISE, AVOCADO, CILANTRO RICE, AND WATERMELON–QUESO FRESCO SALAD

SERVES 4

Another summer meal that'll have you wishing for a fry-an-egg-on-the-sidewalk day. These raw tuna sliders are irresistible. Buy your fish from a reputable fishmonger and tell them you want sushi grade—make sure they know you're going to eat the fish raw. Don't be surprised if they go to the back to get the freshest, best fish. They'll charge you a little extra for it, but when you take your first bite, you won't mind. Wash down this meal with Mexican beer served over ice with a big squeeze of lime.

1 LB/455 G SUSHI-GRADE YELLOWFIN TUNA, MINCED (NOT GROUND)

KOSHER SALT

1 EGG YOLK

12 SLIDER BUNS, 2½ IN/6 CM IN DIAMETER (OR STANDARD BUNS, CUT WITH A BISCUIT CUTTER)

1 TBSP CHOPPED CHIPOTLE CHILE IN ADOBO SAUCE

1 TBSP FRESH LIME JUICE

½ CUP/120 ML MUSTARD AÏOLI (PAGE 90) WITHOUT THE MUSTARD OR FULL-FAT STORE-BOUGHT MAYONNAISE

1 AVOCADO, PITTED, PEELED, AND SLICED

CILANTRO RICE (RECIPE FOLLOWS)

WATERMELON–QUESO FRESCO SALAD (RECIPE FOLLOWS)

Preheat the oven to 350°F/180°C/gas 4. In a medium mixing bowl, combine the tuna, 1 tsp salt, and the egg yolk. Mix thoroughly and form into golf-ball-size rounds. This is most easily done with a scoop—even an ice-cream scoop will do if you don't have anything smaller. Once you've formed the balls, roll each one between your palms to solidify it before placing it on a large dinner plate

(or two). When the balls are formed, cover tightly with plastic wrap and press down lightly to flatten into patties to fit your buns. Refrigerate.

Toast the buns in the oven for 10 to 12 minutes or just until brown on the edges. Remove from the oven and allow to cool. While the buns toast, mix together the chopped chile in adobo sauce, lime juice, and aïoli in a small bowl.

Build the sliders by smearing the sliced avocado over the bottom of the bun and then a generous coating of the chipotle mayonnaise on top of the avocado. Fill with a tuna patty. Bring the sliders to the table on a big platter, accompanied by bowls of Cilantro Rice and the Watermelon-Queso Fresco Salad.

FISH NOTE:
Look for troll- or pole-caught yellowfin, bigeye, or skipjack from Alaska and the U.S. Atlantic. Never buy bluefin—wild or ranched.

— CILANTRO RICE —

Bright, turf green, and flavorful. With this meal, I like to serve this rice at room temperature, but that's up to you.

1½ CUPS/285 G LONG-GRAIN RICE

1⅓ CUPS/315 ML WATER

1 TBSP FRESH LIME JUICE

1 CUP COARSELY CHOPPED FRESH CILANTRO

4 TBSP/55 G BUTTER, MELTED

½ TSP KOSHER SALT

Rinse the rice under cool water until the water runs clear. Drain the rice and combine it with the water in a medium pot with a tight-fitting lid. Set over medium heat and cook for 10 to 12 minutes or until the rice is tender and the water has been absorbed.

In a blender combine the lime juice, cilantro, butter, and salt. Blend until smooth. Pour the cilantro mixture over the rice, mix thoroughly, and serve.

— WATERMELON-QUESO FRESCO SALAD —

As good as watermelon is eaten right off the rind, its place in salads is underappreciated. If you're buying a half melon that's already been cut up, look for dark red pieces. When you make the salad, mix it up. Feel free to add mint or chives or to use feta rather than *queso fresco*. You really can't go wrong.

2¼ LB/1 KG WATERMELON, CUT INTO BITE-SIZE SHARDS

10 OZ/280 G QUESO FRESCO

2 TBSP VERY GOOD EXTRA-VIRGIN OLIVE OIL

FLAKY OR COARSE SALT AND BLACK PEPPER

Combine the watermelon and *queso fresco* in a large serving bowl. Toss with the olive oil and plenty of black pepper. Sprinkle with salt just before serving.

YELLOWFIN TUNA
WITH JALAPEÑO-CUMIN BUTTER AND BUTTERNUT—GOAT CHEESE SALAD

SERVES 4

This recipe is a good example of why I write my books the way I do—with side dishes and main dishes together. The tuna goes so well with the butter, but the combination of the tuna, butter, squash, and goat cheese *all together* is what makes the whole meal reverberate.

¼ CUP/60 ML PEANUT OR VEGETABLE OIL

FOUR 6-OZ/170-G YELLOWFIN TUNA STEAKS, APPROXIMATELY 1 IN/2.5 CM THICK

2 TSP KOSHER SALT

2 TBSP CUMIN SEEDS

JALAPEÑO-CUMIN BUTTER (RECIPE FOLLOWS)

4 LIME WEDGES

Preheat the oven to 175°F/80°C. Use a dab of the oil to rub the tuna steaks all over and liberally salt both sides. Sprinkle one side of the tuna with the cumin seeds. Heat one large cast-iron pan over high heat. Let the pan get very hot before adding the oil. Once you do add the oil, wait for it to shimmer before you put the tuna steaks in the pan, cumin-side up. Cook for 3 to 4 minutes and turn. Cook the cumin-coated side of the tuna for just 1 minute. Transfer to a plate and place 1 tbsp of the Jalapeño-Cumin Butter on each portion before resting it for 3 minutes in the warming oven. Finish with a squeeze of lime.

FISH NOTE:
Buy troll- or pole-caught yellowfin tuna from U.S. or Canadian waters. Substitute mahi mahi. Don't ever buy bluefin—ranched or wild.

⇨

— JALAPEÑO-CUMIN BUTTER —

Toasted cumin mixed with jalapeño and butter. I adore
these flavors and I think you will, too, when you taste
them melted into your fish.

4 TBSP/55 G BUTTER, AT ROOM TEMPERATURE

1 SHALLOT, CHOPPED

2 TBSP CUMIN SEEDS, TOASTED (SEE PAGE 30)
AND GROUND

1 TBSP CORIANDER SEEDS, TOASTED AND GROUND

1 JALAPEÑO WITH SEEDS, MINCED (3 TBSP)

In a small bowl, mash together the butter, shallot, cumin seeds,
coriander seeds, and jalapeño. Set aside.

— BUTTERNUT-GOAT CHEESE SALAD —

Sometimes you just nail a recipe without really expecting to.
I reject plenty of my attempts at combinations of flavors and textures, but this one was a hit the minute I tasted it.

1 LARGE BUTTERNUT SQUASH, PEELED AND CUBED
(ABOUT 6 CUPS/850 G)

1/2 CUP/120 ML OLIVE OIL

2 TSP KOSHER SALT

2 TBSP CIDER VINEGAR

2 OZ/55 G FRESH GOAT CHEESE, CRUMBLED

5 OZ/140 G ARUGULA

FLAKY OR COARSE SALT AND BLACK PEPPER

1/4 CUP/10 G CHOPPED FRESH MINT

Preheat the oven to 400°F/200°C/gas 6. In a mixing bowl, toss the
squash together with half of the olive oil and the kosher salt.
Spread out on a baking sheet in a single layer and roast for 10 to
15 minutes or until the squash is soft and showing spots of black
on the edges. (Really!) In a small bowl, whisk together the remaining
olive oil with the vinegar. Set aside. Combine the goat cheese and
arugula in a large salad bowl. When you're ready to eat, lightly
dress the salad—you won't need all the dressing. Add the butternut
squash, a pinch of flaky or coarse salt, and plenty of black pepper.
Toss, sprinkle on the mint, and serve.

SPICE-RUBBED ARCTIC CHAR
WITH CAULIFLOWER PURÉE AND CHILE ASPARAGUS

SERVES 4

I advise cooking this meal in early spring, when the first asparagus are showing up in the farmers' markets and the cauliflower—grown all winter in California—is pure white and unblemished by the heat. Because I've added a hint of spice to the rub and to the asparagus, you'll find everything on the plate bright and alive.

1 TSP GROUND CUMIN	FOUR 5-OZ/140-G ARCTIC CHAR FILLETS
1 TSP GROUND CORIANDER	1 TBSP OLIVE OR VEGETABLE OIL
1 TSP KOSHER SALT	FLAKY OR COARSE SALT

Preheat the oven to 325°F/165°C/gas 3. In a small bowl, combine the cumin, coriander, and kosher salt. Working on the surface of the butcher paper the fish came wrapped in, coat the fish on both sides with a light slick of oil (I use my hands), and then sprinkle on the spice mixture. Don't go too heavy—you might even have some left over.

Lay a large piece of foil on a baking sheet and put the fillets in the center, leaving about 1 in/2.5 cm between them, and crimping the edges of the foil up to fit the fish. (The foil catches the juice, keeping it near the fish and preventing it from evaporating on the surface of the hot baking sheet.) Cook the fish for 8 to 12 minutes, depending on how thick it is. Beware: the surface or skin may appear uncooked, but the meat will be cooked. You can use a thermometer if you have one—look for 125°F/52°C. Portion out the fish, and put a scoop of the Cauliflower Purée in the center of each plate. Surround with the Chile Asparagus. Add a pinch of flaky or coarse salt, and serve.

FISH NOTE:
Arctic char is a sustainable, farmed fish. Substitute wild Alaskan salmon or coho salmon. Avoid: farm-raised Atlantic salmon.

— CAULIFLOWER PURÉE —

In my first cookbook, *The New Steak*, I came up with a cauliflower mash recipe that I've since made with almost laughable regularity. It's worthy in its own right, but also makes a healthy substitute for mashed potatoes. Here's my latest version, this time with olive oil instead of butter and a bit of that Spice Rub for a pop of extra flavor.

1 HEAD CAULIFLOWER, BROKEN INTO THUMB-SIZE FLORETS

2 TBSP OLIVE OIL

½ TSP KOSHER SALT

½ TSP GROUND CORIANDER

½ TSP GROUND CUMIN

Place a steamer basket in a medium pot with a tight-fitting lid, fill with water to the bottom of the basket, and place over medium-high heat. When the water boils, add the cauliflower and cook for 11 minutes. Remove the cauliflower from the steamer and place in a food processor with the blade attachment in place. Add the olive oil, salt, coriander, and cumin, and process for 1 to 3 minutes—how long depends on the doneness of the cauliflower. The cauliflower should be light and airy, with no lumps. Serve with a generous pinch of the spice rub on top.

— CHILE ASPARAGUS —

Most people eat asparagus with the same accompaniments—egg, mayonnaise, or Parmesan cheese—and I love those things, too. Sometimes I'm in the mood for something different, though, and the chile in this recipe is a revelation.

1 LARGE BUNCH ASPARAGUS

2 TBSP BUTTER

1 SERRANO CHILE, CUT INTO ROUNDS

¼ TSP KOSHER SALT

Trim the asparagus by holding the ends of each spear and bending until it snaps, reserving only the top half and discarding the tougher bottom half. Melt the butter in a large sauté pan over high heat. Add the asparagus, chile, and salt to the pan. Cook for 3 to 8 minutes or until the butter is well browned, the chiles are lightly browned, and the asparagus spears have lost their raw flavor. How long they take to cook will depend on how thick they are and how hot your burner is. Taste for salt and serve hot.

PANFRIED LIME-CHIPOTLE TILAPIA
WITH CHILE CORN

SERVES 4

Tilapia is an honest workhorse—it's an affordable, versatile fish that's farmed using sustainable methods in the United States and the European Union. It has a mild flavor and an appealing flakiness. Fish snobs complain about it, but don't join their ranks until you've cooked it yourself. This easy recipe is a good place to start. I like to spoon plenty of the spicy, acidic lime-chipotle sauce onto my plate so I can eat it with the Chile Corn. Rice of any kind (the Cilantro Rice on page 113 would be ideal) or a steaming cloth with warm tortillas will pair nicely with the fish. Some greens would not be unwelcome here.

JUICE OF 2 LIMES

1 LARGE TOMATO, CORED AND MINCED

2 OR 3 CHIPOTLE CHILES IN ADOBO SAUCE

2 TSP KOSHER SALT

1 TBSP OLIVE OIL

1 1/2 LB/680 G TILAPIA FILLETS

1/2 CUP/120 ML VEGETABLE OR PEANUT OIL

2 1/2 CUPS/325 G UNBLEACHED ALL-PURPOSE FLOUR

1/4 CUP/10 G COARSELY CHOPPED FRESH CILANTRO

FLAKY OR COARSE SALT

CHILE CORN (RECIPE FOLLOWS)

In a small serving bowl, combine the juice of 1 lime, tomato, chipotle chiles, 1 tsp of the kosher salt, and the olive oil and set aside. Pour the remaining juice of 1 lime and the 1 tsp kosher salt in a shallow dish. Coat the fish with it on both sides. Allow the fish to marinate for at least 30 minutes and up to 3 hours in the refrigerator.

Preheat the oven to 175°F/80°C. Heat the vegetable oil in a large, deep frying pan until it is just smoking or reaches 385°F/196°C on a thermometer. Put the flour in a shallow dish. Dredge the fish in the flour and lay it carefully in the vegetable oil. Cook for 3 to 5 minutes on the first side and for 1 to 3 minutes on the second side. You're going for a nicely browned, crusty exterior. Work in batches as needed, transferring the cooked fish to a plate in the warming oven. When all the fish is done, sprinkle with a little flaky or coarse salt and serve with the Chile Corn and plenty of the lime-chipotle sauce.

FISH NOTE:
Tilapia is a sustainable farm-raised fish when bought from a U.S. or E.U. fish farm. Avoid: all imported farmed fish from Asia, and be wary of South American farmed fish. Substitute whatever is freshest at the market—this is a supremely versatile recipe.

— CHILE CORN —

Even when combined with frozen corn in winter, the chile, coriander, and cumin deliver a lively, surprising side dish. Make this recipe with fresh, young corn in summer, and you may be done with eating corn straight off the cob for quite some time.

1 TBSP OLIVE OIL

1 SERRANO CHILE

1 TBSP CORIANDER SEEDS, CRUSHED WITH THE SIDE OF A LARGE KNIFE OR IN A SMALL MORTAR AND PESTLE

1 TSP CUMIN SEEDS, TOASTED (SEE PAGE 30)

3 CUPS/360 G FRESH CORN KERNELS, SHAVED OFF THE COB (ABOUT 6 EARS)

KOSHER SALT

Heat the olive oil in a large sauté pan over medium-high heat. Add the chile, coriander seeds, and cumin seeds and cook for 2 to 3 minutes or until the chile begins to color slightly. Add the corn and cook for 2 to 3 minutes or until just heated through. Season with salt.

CENOTE FISH TACOS
WITH TOMATILLO-RADISH SALSA AND CILANTRO CORN

SERVES 4

Cenotes are cave openings where an underground river has popped through to the earth's surface. They can be found throughout the Yucatán Peninsula (and elsewhere). Swimming in this fresh, clear blue water with the tiny fish that dwell here is an experience not to be missed. These tacos are inspired by my family's most recent trip to Mexico. No contest: the best things about our days there were these simple, fresh tacos and finding our bodies once again moving through the cool blue water of a cenote.

16 TO 20 SMALL CORN TORTILLAS

6 OZ/170 G QUESO FRESCO, CRUMBLED

1 CUP/240 ML MEXICAN CREMA (SUBSTITUTE FULL-FAT SOUR CREAM)

2 HASS AVOCADOS, PITTED, PEELED, AND DICED

2 TSP FRESH LIME JUICE

1½ TSP KOSHER SALT

1 LB/455 G U.S. FARMED CATFISH

1 EGG

1 CUP/130 G ALL-PURPOSE FLOUR

½ CUP/70 G CORNMEAL

¼ TSP CAYENNE PEPPER

¼ CUP/60 ML PEANUT OR VEGETABLE OIL

FLAKY OR COARSE SALT

TOMATILLO-RADISH SALSA (RECIPE FOLLOWS)

CILANTRO CORN (RECIPE FOLLOWS)

Preheat the oven to 200°F/95°C. Spread out a sheet of aluminum foil. Dash a little water on it with your hands—maybe a teaspoonful. Wrap the stacked tortillas tightly in the foil, crimping the edges carefully so that no air can get in, and put them in the oven. Put the crumbled cheese and the *crema* in two pretty bowls, cover, and refrigerate. Toss the avocados with the lime juice and ½ tsp of the kosher salt. Cover and set aside.

Cut the fish into finger-size pieces. Crack the egg into a medium bowl and beat. Put the flour, remaining 1 tsp of kosher salt, cornmeal, and cayenne into another medium bowl. Heat the oil over medium-high heat in a large frying pan—ideally cast iron. Dip the fish, in batches, in the egg and then in the flour before placing it in the hot oil. Cook for 2 to 3 minutes on each side, depending on the thickness of the fish. When it's done, sprinkle the fish with a pinch of flaky or coarse salt and transfer to a plate. Place the plate in the oven with the tortillas.

When you're ready to eat, bring the *queso*, *crema*, avocados, Tomatillo-Radish Salsa, tortillas (wrap them up in a napkin, if you like), fish, and Cilantro Corn to the table. Pass and build your tacos, taking care not to overfill. The Cilantro Corn is delicious in the taco—but it's really meant to be a side. Maybe a bit on the plate and a bit in the taco is the way to go.

FISH NOTE:
Buy only U.S. farmed catfish. Alternatively, you can substitute pretty much any other seafood—although I've never had a clam or oyster taco, I'm sure it would be tasty! Avoid: imported catfish from China or other parts of Asia.

— TOMATILLO-RADISH SALSA —

The tomatillo's citrus-scented presence is always welcome on my plate. Mixed with radishes, as here, its pretty green color and unexpected brightness carry the salsa from plain to glorious.

8 OZ/225 G TOMATILLOS, PEELED

8 FRENCH BREAKFAST RADISHES, TRIMMED

3 GREEN ONIONS, WHITE AND TENDER GREEN PARTS, THINLY SLICED

½ CUP/20 G CHOPPED FRESH CILANTRO

2 GARLIC CLOVES, MINCED

1 SERRANO CHILE, MINCED, WITH SEEDS

1 TSP KOSHER SALT

1 TBSP FRESH LIME JUICE

1 TSP CUMIN SEEDS, TOASTED (SEE PAGE 30) AND LIGHTLY CRUSHED

Fill a medium bowl with cold water. Bring a medium pot filled with water to a boil and blanch the tomatillos for 1 minute, immediately transferring them to the cold water to cool. Drain, pat dry, core, and coarsely chop. Thinly slice the radishes, then cut across the slices to create small batons. In a pretty serving bowl, mix together the tomatillos, radishes, green onions, cilantro, garlic, chile, salt, lime juice, and cumin seeds. Taste for salt and heat. The salsa will mellow as it sits.

— CILANTRO CORN —

This is really double-cilantro corn. The recipe contains both the seed—coriander—and the fresh leaf of the plant. It's a great combination. The quality of your olive oil and your corn matter. If you don't have fresh corn, use frozen corn with great olive oil.

¼ CUP/60 ML EXTRA-VIRGIN OLIVE OIL

3½ CUPS/595 G FRESH CORN KERNELS, SHAVED OFF THE COB (ABOUT 8 EARS OF FRESH CORN; IN WINTER, SUBSTITUTE FROZEN)

1 TBSP CORIANDER SEEDS, LIGHTLY CRUSHED

½ TSP KOSHER SALT

¼ CUP/10 G CHOPPED FRESH CILANTRO

FLAKY OR COARSE SALT

Heat the olive oil in a large sauté pan over high heat. Add the corn, coriander seeds, and kosher salt and cook for 5 to 10 minutes, stirring frequently. If you have local corn in the summer, simply heat it through. If you're using frozen corn, cook for 8 to 10 minutes. When the corn is cooked to your liking, add the cilantro, stir, taste for salt, and serve with a pinch of flaky or coarse salt.

LOS GATOS CEVICHE,
LIME-TORTILLA SOUP,
AND GUACAMOLE WITH
HANDMADE CHIPS

SERVES 4

This meal is an ideal complement to a rowdy evening of drinking and talking. (A rowdy afternoon works, too.) Make plenty of chips and guacamole, because you'll see them disappear quickly. As for the ceviche, you'll be eating raw fish, so you'll want to buy the freshest fish from a trusted source.

¼ CUP/60 ML FRESH LEMON JUICE
(ABOUT 1 LEMON)

¼ CUP FRESH LIME JUICE
(ABOUT 2 LIMES)

2 TBSP FRESH ORANGE JUICE

10 SCALLOPS (ABOUT 1 LB/455 G), CUT INTO
DICE-SIZE CUBES

12 OZ/340 G WHITE FISH, SKINNED AND CUT INTO
DICE-SIZE CUBES

1 SERRANO CHILE, MINCED

1 TOMATO, FINELY CHOPPED, SOLIDS ONLY

¼ CUP/10 G FINELY CHOPPED FRESH CILANTRO

KOSHER SALT (OPTIONAL)

In a small, pretty bowl combine the lemon juice, lime juice, and orange juice with the scallops, fish (or all fish, if that's what you're using), chile, tomato, and cilantro. Cover and set the bowl in the refrigerator to marinate for 25 to 30 minutes. Don't over-"cook" in the acid. If needed, season with the salt. Eat the ceviche on its own. (Consider eating with chips or portioning out the Lime-Tortilla Soup in bowls and then composing a little plate with a portion of chips, guacamole, and ceviche for each person at the table. Family style works, too.)

Red snapper is traditional, but it has been fished heavily. Look
for gray snapper. Scallops are a natural, but shrimp, cod, white
sea bass, and Pacific or North Atlantic haddock work beautifully,
too. In fact, use any nonoily saltwater fish—you don't want
sardines, salmon, bluefish, or mackerel.

— LIME-TORTILLA SOUP —

When it's in front of me, I find it difficult to pay attention
to anything—or anyone—else. Maybe it's those rich avocados, the
still-crispy chips, and spicy, lime-scented broth.

2 TBSP OLIVE, PEANUT, OR VEGETABLE OIL

1 SWEET ONION, SUCH AS VIDALIA, CHOPPED

3 TO 6 GARLIC CLOVES, DEPENDING ON SIZE,
THINLY SLICED

1 TO 2 FRESH HOT CHILES, SUCH AS JALAPEÑO,
SERRANO, OR ARBOL, CUT INTO THIN ROUNDS
(KEEP THE SEEDS FOR THE BEST HEAT)

1 TSP CUMIN SEEDS

2 TOMATOES, CHOPPED

KOSHER SALT

5 CUPS/1.2 L CHICKEN OR FISH STOCK (PAGE 27)

2 CUPS/240 G FRESH CORN KERNELS, SHAVED OFF
THE COB (ABOUT 4 EARS)

2 LIMES, 1 JUICED AND 1 CUT INTO WEDGES

1 AVOCADO, PITTED, PEELED, AND DICED

HANDMADE CHIPS (RECIPE FOLLOWS)

1/2 CUP/20 G CHOPPED FRESH CILANTRO

1/4 CUP/60 ML MEXICAN CREMA OR SOUR CREAM

GUACAMOLE (RECIPE FOLLOWS)

In a large pot you will cook the soup in, combine the oil, onion,
garlic, chiles, and cumin seeds. Set the pot over medium heat and
cook for 5 to 8 minutes or until the onion is soft. Stir often to
prevent the garlic from burning. Add the tomatoes, 1 tsp of salt,
the stock, and the corn. Bring to a boil, turn down the heat, and
simmer gently for 5 to 8 minutes. Add the lime juice, stir, and taste
for salt and heat. In a small bowl, toss the avocado with salt.

Line four soup bowls with Handmade Chips and pour the broth on
top. Top each serving with cilantro, 1 wedge of lime, chips, and
crema. Eat with chips dipped in guacamole or in ceviche—maybe
both. Scatter more chips on your soup, as you please.

— GUACAMOLE —

I like to keep it simple when it comes to Guacamole. Lime juice, a
tiny bit of garlic, and salt. Serve this at room temperature.

2 TBSP FRESH LIME JUICE   1½ TSP MINCED GARLIC

1 TSP KOSHER SALT   4 HASS AVOCADOS, PITTED, PEELED, AND SLICED

In a small serving bowl, combine the lime juice, salt, and garlic.
Add the avocado and mash with a fork until it's smooth. Use a salty
chip to taste for salt before serving.

— HANDMADE CHIPS —

These are so much better than store-bought chips. The experience is
not unlike eating *beurre blanc* and then finally making it yourself, only to witness the obscene quantity of butter that goes into
it. Look away as you fry these chips.

2 CUPS/480 ML PEANUT OR VEGETABLE OIL   KOSHER SALT

15 TO 20 SMALL CORN TORTILLAS, CUT INTO STRIPS
THE WIDTH OF YOUR PINKY

Split the oil between two large frying pans (or use one, but it'll
take twice as long). Set the pans over medium heat and bring the oil
to 350°F/180°C. If you don't have a deep-fat thermometer, test the oil
by ripping off a piece of a tortilla. If the tortilla browns on one
side within 2 minutes, the oil is hot enough. Put a handful of the
tortilla pieces in the hot oil, allowing them to overlap slightly.
They should brown within 1 to 2 minutes. Stir the chips around to
be sure both sides are browned. Use a slotted spoon or spatula to
transfer the cooked chips to a paper towel-lined baking sheet. Add
a pinch of salt while the chips are still hot.

GARLIC SHRIMP,
RED RICE, BLACK BEANS, AND
ROASTED PADRÓN CHILES

SERVES 4

Garlic and shrimp are a venerable combination. Best of all, this slow-cooking method mellows the garlic without taking away its pungency. You'll have the unalloyed joy of a garlic hit, with rich Black Beans, Roasted Padrón Chiles, and Red Rice. A drink involving tequila would not be out of place.

3 TBSP BUTTER	FLAKY OR COARSE SALT
1/2 HEAD GARLIC, PEELED AND CHOPPED	1/2 CUP/120 ML SOUR CREAM OR MEXICAN CREMA
1 1/2 LB/680 G SHRIMP, PEELED AND DEVEINED	RED RICE (RECIPE FOLLOWS)
1/2 TSP CHILE FLAKES	BLACK BEANS (RECIPE FOLLOWS)
4 TO 6 GREEN ONIONS, THINLY SLICED	ROASTED PADRÓN CHILES (RECIPE FOLLOWS)
2 TBSP FRESH LIME JUICE	1/4 CUP/10 G CHOPPED FRESH CILANTRO

Combine the butter and garlic over very low heat. Allow the butter to soften without getting very hot for 3 to 5 minutes. Keep the heat on low, add the shrimp and chile flakes, and cook slowly with the garlic for 5 to 8 minutes, depending on the size of the shrimp and your heat source. When the shrimp are done—taste one—add the lime juice and adjust for salt, as needed.

To make the plates, put a spoonful of rice and beans next to each other in the center of a plate. Put the shrimp on top of the rice and a good dollop of sour cream on the beans. Surround the plate with the roasted chiles. Sprinkle everything on the plate with cilantro and serve.

FISH NOTE:
Buy U.S. farmed or wild-caught shrimp. Alaskan spot prawns and
pink shrimp from Oregon are sustainable and very tasty. Avoid:
farm-raised shrimp from China and other Asian countries, including
India, Malaysia, and Thailand.

— RED RICE —

Memorably spiced and pretty to boot.

1 CUP/215 G BASMATI RICE

1 ⅓ CUPS/315 ML WATER

½ TSP KOSHER SALT

2 TBSP OLIVE OIL OR BUTTER

1 ONION, FINELY CHOPPED

1 TOMATO, FINELY CHOPPED

1 TSP GROUND CORIANDER

½ TSP ANCHO CHILE POWDER

1 SERRANO CHILE, MINCED

Rinse the rice under cool water until the water no longer appears
cloudy. In a medium pot with a tight-fitting lid, combine the rice,
water, and salt. Cook for 10 to 12 minutes or until the rice is
tender and the water has been absorbed.

While the rice is cooking, in a medium sauté pan set over medium
heat, combine the oil and onion. Cook for 5 to 8 minutes or until
the onion is soft. Add the tomato, coriander, chile powder, and chile.
Cook for 5 to 8 minutes or until the tomato has released some of its
moisture, that moisture has evaporated, and the whole mixture has
begun to stick to the pan. Fluff the rice gently with a fork, and
then add the tomato mixture without overmixing. Season with additional salt as needed.

— BLACK BEANS —

Dried beans cooked on the stove top with a little onion, garlic,
and cumin seeds are worlds apart from canned. Don't worry if you
haven't soaked the beans—I never do. They'll take about an hour
straight out of the bag, so plan accordingly.

2 TBSP VEGETABLE OIL, OLIVE OIL, OR BUTTER

2 GARLIC CLOVES, CRUSHED

1 TBSP CUMIN SEEDS

1 ONION, COARSELY CHOPPED

2¼ CUPS/450 G DRIED BLACK BEANS

7 TO 8 CUPS/1.7 TO 2 L WATER

1 TSP KOSHER SALT

In a pot with a tight-fitting lid, combine the oil, garlic, cumin
seeds, and onion and set over medium heat for 5 to 8 minutes. Stir
often to prevent the onion and garlic from sticking or burning.
When the onion is softened and the cumin is fragrant, add the
beans and 7 cups/1.7 L of water, cover, and set over low heat for
40 minutes. After 40 minutes, uncover the pot and stir the beans. Be
sure there is plenty of liquid remaining so that the beans don't
scorch. Watch them, stirring often, for the next 20 minutes or until
they are tender and the water has been absorbed. Add a little more
water if you need to. Add the salt, taste, and adjust the consistency
of the beans by adding more water if they are too stiff. I like them
with some liquid so they aren't dry.

— ROASTED PADRÓN CHILES —

Two bites that vary from slightly to very fiery, these chiles are
memorable and well worth the hunt. I grow them so I always have
a supply, but you can find them at farmers' markets and good
grocery stores. Look for shishito peppers as a substitute—
they're equally good.

1 1/2 LB/680 G PADRÓN CHILES

1 TBSP OLIVE OIL

1/2 TSP KOSHER SALT

FLAKY OR COARSE SALT

Preheat the oven to 500°F/260°C/gas 10. In a mixing bowl, toss the
chiles with the olive oil and kosher salt, coating them thoroughly. Spread out the chiles on a baking sheet and roast for
8 to 12 minutes or until the chiles show flecks of black. Finish
with a pinch of flaky or coarse salt.

CHAPTER 4

EAST ASIAN FISH

EAST ASIAN FISH

You'll want to stock up on cilantro, mint, fresh ginger, Thai full-fat coconut milk, fish sauce made in Thailand or Vietnam, chili paste (I like Lao Luo Zi brand, Chaotian Chili from Taiwan, but the more common Huy Fong Foods is just fine), plus some fresh chiles. You'll also want to have some mirin, rice vinegar, soy sauce, rice wine, and sriracha handy. And you won't mind having bonito flakes and seaweed—wakame and roasted shredded seaweed flakes—along with rice noodles and udon noodles. All of these seemingly exotic (if you don't cook this way) ingredients can be easily found at an Asian grocery store. If you've never been to one of these emporiums, it's time. You'll thank me.

DRINKS

Tsingtao remains my favorite widely available Asian beer. Of course, nothing is stopping you from drinking whatever's local—that's what I do. Fill up a growler at the local pub and finish it before it goes flat. If beer isn't your thing, drink a relatively inexpensive white wine. Steer clear of reds, especially those with heavy tannins. Consider instead an icy Vinho Verde, a dry Riesling, or a well-chilled rosé. Don't drink subtle wine with the food in this chapter—all that spice will make it difficult to appreciate.

AT THE TABLE

Another style of food that lends itself to a rowdy feast, with plenty of small, colorful bowls and various textures and flavors eaten side by side—spicy, sweet, sour, bitter. Bring a pot of jasmine rice to the table, unadulterated. It'll provide a welcome antidote to all that fiery food. That said, provide the means for those who wish to make their food spicier: A jar of Smoky Sweet Hot Sauce (page 211) will do the trick, and so will simple minced chiles. Cut limes or lemons to squeeze for an extra hit of acid are never a bad idea, and neither is a little pot of soy in lieu of flaky or coarse salt, if the recipe is not Chinese. Make your table pretty with a crazy number of low tea lights to shed an exotic light on your meal.

SWEETS

Keep it simple. Cut up a ripe mango and put the chunks on skewers. Squeeze lime juice over the fruit and then add a pinch of coarse or flaky salt. Melon is also splendid this way. For a more involved dessert, I like to cook rice pudding or large-pearl tapioca using coconut milk. Go easy on the sugar, so the pudding is not overly sweet, and don't forget the salt. Finish with toasted grated coconut and a splash of black rum.

FISH ON A STICK
WITH SPICY PEANUT DIPPING SAUCE, DAN DAN NOODLES, AND WATERMELON-CUCUMBER SALAD

SERVES 4

I feel certain Huck and Jim ate fish on a stick, out there on their raft in the grand Mississippi. Mark Twain wrote about a catfish that "was as big as a man" and caught with a "skinned rabbit" for bait. I doubt you'll be catching your own, much less one as big as you are. Whether the "meat's white as snow" as Huck and Jim's was, it should be fresh and firm so it stays on that stick. I recommend catfish, tilapia, or mahi mahi. Put together with those spicy noodles and refreshing salad, this is my kind of food.

1½ LB/680 G CATFISH, TILAPIA, OR MAHI MAHI, CUT INTO ROUGH 1½-IN/4-CM CHUNKS (THEY WON'T BE SQUARE; DON'T WORRY)

¼ CUP/60 ML SOY SAUCE

2 TBSP VEGETABLE OR PEANUT OIL

SPICY PEANUT DIPPING SAUCE (RECIPE FOLLOWS)

DAN DAN NOODLES (RECIPE FOLLOWS)

WATERMELON-CUCUMBER SALAD (RECIPE FOLLOWS)

Put the fish chunks in a medium mixing bowl with the soy sauce and oil. Put the bowl in the refrigerator and marinate the fish for at least 10 minutes or up to 1 hour. Thread the fish onto either metal skewers or wood skewers that have been soaked in water for at least 1 hour. The fish should not be tightly packed on the skewer, but the chunks should be touching. Preheat the broiler to high with the rack 3 to 4 in/7.5 to 10 cm from the heat source. Line a baking sheet with foil, and place the fish on it so the skewers are close but not touching. Crimp the sides up to catch the juices, and place the fish under the broiler.

Cook the fish for 5 to 6 minutes, depending on how thick the pieces are. Try to pull one of the largest pieces off a skewer—it should pull right off. Transfer the cooked fish, still on the skewers, to plates. Pour any juices captured in the foil over the fish. Toss the noodles with half of the Spicy Peanut Dipping Sauce. Put the remainder of the sauce in a couple of small serving bowls. Round out the plate with the noodles and salad.

<u>FISH NOTE:</u>
Buy U.S. or E.U. farm-raised catfish, or U.S. or E.U. farm-raised tilapia. Avoid: Asian catfish, all imported farmed fish from Asia, and be wary of South American farmed fish.

— SPICY PEANUT DIPPING SAUCE —

One of the limitations of Western cooking is its failure to use peanuts in savory dishes. We have peanut butter cookies, sandwiches, pies, and brittle but hardly a peanut sauce in our repertoire. Forget the sweet and bring on the salt and spice.

¼ CUP/25 G CHILE FLAKES	3 HEAPING TBSP UNSWEETENED PEANUT BUTTER
2 TBSP PEANUT OIL	2 TSP SICHUAN PEPPER, FINELY CRUSHED
3 TBSP SOY SAUCE	6 GREEN ONIONS, FINELY CHOPPED

Combine the ingredients in a small bowl and mix.

— DAN DAN NOODLES —

I know it's heresy to put Korean kimchi in Dan Dan noodles, but I do it anyway because I always have a jar of kimchi hiding in my refrigerator. (It's smokin' good on a hot dog with a little squirt of sriracha, but I digress.) Kimchi or Asian vegetables aside, these noodles are surprising and crazy-delicious.

1 TBSP PEANUT OIL

3 SERRANO CHILES, MINCED

½ TSP SICHUAN PEPPER, CRUSHED

4 OZ/115 G BACON, MINCED

½ CUP/40 G KIMCHI OR OTHER PICKLED VEGETABLE (I LIKE TOBAGI BRAND KIMCHI)

3 TSP SOY SAUCE

12 OZ/340 G DRIED CHINESE NOODLES (SUBSTITUTE FRESH EGG NOODLES), COOKED AS DIRECTED ON THE PACKAGE

½ RECIPE SPICY PEANUT DIPPING SAUCE (PAGE 139)

Heat a wok or large frying pan over medium-high heat. When the pan is hot, add the peanut oil, chiles, Sichuan pepper, and bacon. Cook, stirring frequently, until the bacon is crispy. Turn the heat down if the oil smokes. As soon as the bacon is cooked, add the kimchi and soy sauce. Cook for another 1 or 2 minutes. Transfer to a serving bowl and toss together with the cooked noodles and the dipping sauce.

— WATERMELON-CUCUMBER SALAD —

This slightly sweet salad is super refreshing and a terrific anti-dote to the Dan Dan Noodle heat.

¼ LARGE WATERMELON, CUT INTO BITE-SIZE CHUNKS OR SHARDS

1 SEEDLESS CUCUMBER, CUT INTO ROUNDS

2 TSP PONZU (SUBSTITUTE LIGHT SOY SAUCE)

2 TSP RICE VINEGAR

1 TBSP OLIVE OIL

Combine the watermelon and cucumber in a serving bowl. Toss with the ponzu, rice vinegar, and olive oil just before serving.

AROMATIC WOK-BRAISED SNAPPER
WITH TATSOI AND JASMINE RICE

SERVES 4

Sometimes I find myself in a slump. For me that means my food tastes too much the same and I catch myself yearning for a quick trip to Shanghai or at least to one of the fabulous dives in New York's Chinatown. On one such night I decided to cook a pretty whole snapper using a method of braising in a wok that I hadn't tried before. Using Chinese ingredients, but not wanting to make anything too complicated, I set to work. The fragrant, spicy result that was on my plate in less than 30 minutes jolted me back to fearless self-confidence. One taste and you'll know you don't need to venture any farther than your own kitchen to get excited about your own food, either.

ONE 1½- TO 2-LB/680- TO 910-G WHOLE GRAY SNAPPER, GUTTED AND SCALED, HEAD LEFT ON

2 TBSP SHAOXING COOKING WINE

2 TBSP SOY SAUCE

2 TBSP CHILI PASTE (LAO LUO ZI'S CHILI PASTE IS TERRIFIC)

1 THUMB-LENGTH PIECE FRESH GINGER, PEELED AND FINELY CHOPPED

2 GARLIC CLOVES, CHOPPED

1 TBSP HOISIN SAUCE

1 TBSP FERMENTED BLACK BEANS

1 TBSP CHINKIANG VINEGAR

¼ CUP/60 ML VEGETABLE OR PEANUT OIL

2 CUPS/480 ML CHICKEN OR FISH STOCK (PAGE 27)

1 TSP CORNSTARCH DISSOLVED IN 1 TSP WATER

8 OZ/225 G TATSOI, COARSELY CHOPPED (SUBSTITUTE BOK CHOY OR BABY SPINACH)

5 GREEN ONIONS, THINLY SLICED

JASMINE RICE (PAGE 155) FOR SERVING

Slash the side of the fish three or four times on each side. Combine the cooking wine and soy sauce in a large mixing bowl. Coat the fish inside and out with the soy mixture, and allow it to sit in the sauce as you ready your other ingredients.

In a small bowl or ramekin, combine the chili paste, ginger, garlic, hoisin, black beans, and vinegar. No need to mix. Set aside. Set a wok over high heat. When it begins to smoke, add the oil, allowing it to heat until shimmering. Remove the fish from the marinade, reserving the leftover marinade, and dry the fish with a paper towel before laying it carefully in the hot oil. Cook for 3 minutes before turning the fish over to brown the other side. It's simplest to grab hold of the tail and turn the fish over carefully. Put on an oven mitt if you're concerned about burning yourself in that hot oil. Once the other side of the fish is browned, transfer the fish to a plate.

Add the reserved bowl of aromatics to the hot oil, taking care not to splatter. Cook over high heat for 2 to 3 minutes or until fragrant. Add the stock, cornstarch, and any leftover marinade to the wok. Stir and then return the fish to the wok. Don't worry if the tail and head stick out of the liquid. The body of the fish should be mostly under the liquid. Cook the fish over high heat for 8 to 10 minutes or until a knife inserted gently into the thickest part meets little resistance and the flesh appears flaky. Carefully remove the fish from the liquid and place on a large, deep platter. Add the tatsoi to the wok and cook for 1 to 2 minutes or until just wilted.

Use a slotted spoon to remove the greens from the broth, arranging them around the fish. Pour the remaining liquid over the fish and finish by sprinkling the green onions over the whole thing. If the platter threatens to overflow, put the remaining liquid in a small pitcher. Serve over rice in flat bowls or deep plates. Use a fork and a small spatula to remove the flesh from the top half of the fish before removing the vertebrae. Watch for bones as you serve and when you're eating. (For more on serving whole fish, see page 23.)

FISH NOTE:
Red snapper is overfished according to the Monterey Bay Aquarium Seafood Watch. Gray snapper is more abundant. Look for fish managed by a solid quota system, as in the Gulf of Mexico. If you don't know where your snapper came from or would rather use a more sustainable fish, look for black bass or black rockfish from U.S. waters.

WOK-BRAISED HADDOCK
WITH CHILES, MINCED PORK, AND SNAP PEAS OVER JASMINE RICE

SERVES 4

There's nothing difficult about this sumptuous, porky stir-fry, despite the lengthy ingredient list. Don't be put off. All you're doing is marinating a piece of fish; browning a little pork in hot oil; using that same oil to heat a bunch of spice pastes, sauces, and garlic; and then adding your fish along with some liquid. To finish you throw in the vegetables and cook them along with everything else. Get the sequence in your head, your *mise en place* in order, and that wok so hot it glows—in that order.

3 TBSP DARK SOY SAUCE

3 TBSP SHAOXING COOKING WINE

1 LB/455 G HADDOCK FILLET, CUT INTO 6 TO 8 PIECES

1 TBSP SHRIMP PASTE WITH BEAN OIL

1 TBSP CHILI PASTE (SUBSTITUTE 1 TO 2 WHOLE CHILES)

2 TBSP HOISIN SAUCE

1 TBSP YELLOW MUSTARD SEEDS

3 GARLIC CLOVES, MINCED

3 TBSP VEGETABLE OR PEANUT OIL

1 PORK CHOP (ABOUT 5 OZ/140 G), DICED

1½ CUPS/360 ML CHICKEN OR FISH STOCK (PAGE 27) OR WATER

12 OZ/340 G SUGAR SNAP PEAS

1 RED BELL PEPPER, SEEDED AND CUT INTO THIN SLIVERS

1 TBSP CORNSTARCH DISSOLVED IN 1 TBSP WATER

2 CUPS/120 G RIBBON-CUT NAPA CABBAGE

JASMINE RICE (PAGE 155)

⅓ CUP/50 G SALTED ROASTED PEANUTS, COARSELY CHOPPED

¼ CUP/25 G CHOPPED GREEN ONIONS

Briefly marinate the fish in a medium mixing bowl by combining the soy sauce, cooking wine, and haddock. Stir to coat the fish. Cover and refrigerate until it goes in the wok or for up to 2 hours.

In a small bowl, combine the shrimp paste, chili paste, hoisin, mustard seeds, and garlic. Set aside.

Heat the wok on your hottest burner on high until the wok is very hot. Add the oil and when it glistens and threatens to smoke, add the pork. Cook the pork until it gets slightly crispy and browns, 3 to 5 minutes. Turn off the heat under the wok and transfer the pork to a small bowl and set it aside, leaving the oil behind in the wok.

Return the wok to high heat and add the reserved mixture of pastes, hoisin sauce, mustard seeds, and garlic. Cook for about 1 minute or until the garlic *just* begins to color. Quickly add the stock and the fish along with its marinade. Settle the fish in the liquid and bring it to a simmer. Cook for 2 to 3 minutes, depending on the thickness of the fish fillets. The fish will not be done all the way through at this point. Add the sugar snaps and the pepper, and cook for 2 more minutes before adding the cornstarch, pork, and cabbage. Cook for 1 to 2 minutes longer. The fish should have flaked apart into the now thickened liquid and the pork should be hot. Serve over Jasmine Rice and sprinkle with chopped peanuts and green onions.

FISH NOTE:
Look for Pacific haddock or Atlantic haddock from the Baltic Sea (Norway or Russia). You could also substitute Pacific cod or Atlantic cod from Iceland, Norway, Canada, or Russia.

WHOLE BAKED BRANZINO
WITH WATERMELON-MANGO RELISH, JASMINE RICE, AND SAUTÉED-GARLIC BOK CHOY

SERVES 4

Watermelon, mango, and fish sauce with garlic- and ginger-rubbed branzino is hot-weather food of the kind that makes you wish for a heat wave. Between the brined sweetness of the fish, a hint of heat, and that fresh, tropical sweetness of the fruit, this dish cools me down and makes me happy every time. Bok choy with lots of garlic and a neat bowl of fragrant jasmine rice on the side, and all I need is a tall, icy boat drink.

½ CUP/20 G FINELY CHOPPED FRESH CILANTRO STEMS AND LEAVES

5 GREEN ONIONS, FINELY CHOPPED

1 SERRANO OR JALAPEÑO CHILE, FINELY CHOPPED

1 THUMB-LENGTH PIECE FRESH GINGER, PEELED AND MINCED

¼ CUP/60 ML LIME JUICE

2 TBSP FISH SAUCE

1 TBSP PEANUT OIL

ONE 2- TO 3-LB/910- TO 1.4-KG WHOLE BRANZINO, GUTTED AND SCALED, HEAD AND TAIL LEFT ON

ONE 6-OZ/170-G PIECE WATERMELON, CUT INTO ½-IN/12-MM CUBES

1 MANGO, PITTED, PEELED, AND CUT INTO ½-IN/12-MM CUBES

JASMINE RICE (PAGE 155)

Preheat the oven to 400°F/200°C/gas 6. Combine the cilantro, green onions, chile, and ginger and divide the mixture in half, placing each half in a separate bowl. Pour half of the lime juice into each bowl. Set one of the bowls aside for the relish. Add the fish sauce and peanut oil to the remaining bowl. Mix well.

Remove the fish from the refrigerator. Be sure it is clean and dry. Rinse and dry the fish again if there is blood on the paper or if the interior looks less than clean. Line a baking sheet with parchment paper and lay the fish on it. With your sharpest knife, make three or four slits down both sides of the fish to score it. Make the slits deep enough so that they go into the flesh of the fish. Take the aromatics-and-fish-sauce mixture and put as much of it as you can into the slits. Rub a little on the skin and add whatever remains to the cavity of the fish.

Bake the fish for 12 to 15 minutes or until the flesh is flaky and no longer opaque. Toss the watermelon, mango, and aromatics-and-lime-juice mixture together in a serving bowl. Serve the fish with the watermelon-mango mixture, the Sautéed-Garlic Bok Choy, and Jasmine Rice. (For more on serving whole fish, see page 23.)

FISH NOTE:
Branzino is a sustainably farmed fish. Substitute E.U. farmed barramundi, trout, or a gray or lane snapper.

— SAUTÉED-GARLIC BOK CHOY —

Bok choy is a mild, easy to love green. Cooked with plenty of garlic, it puts me in mind of a day in New York City's Chinatown and the irresistible bowls of greens that arrive at the table in a cloud of their own aromatic steam.

2 TBSP OLIVE OIL	¼ CUP/60 ML WATER
½ HEAD GARLIC, CLOVES PEELED AND SLICED	1 TBSP SOY SAUCE
5 BABY OR 2 MATURE HEADS BOK CHOY, TRIMMED AND COARSELY CHOPPED	FLAKY OR COARSE SALT

Put the oil in a large frying pan with a lid over medium heat. Add the garlic and let it cook for about 1 minute before adding the bok choy along with the water and soy sauce. Stir to coat the bok choy with oil and to move the garlic around. Cover and cook for 3 to 5 minutes. Remove the lid, taste, and cook for another 2 minutes or so or until the greens are tender and the pan is nearly dry. Sprinkle with a pinch of flaky or coarse salt and serve.

RAMEN NOODLE BOWL:
HAKE, PULLED PORK, POACHED EGG, BEET, GREEN ONIONS, AND DAIKON IN RICH BROTH

SERVES 4

This dazzling soup will slow down even the fastest noodle-eater. If you have a source for good pulled pork, use it. If not, make your own by rubbing a pork butt with equal parts sugar and salt and cooking it at 200°F/95°C for 4 to 6 hours. Don't be shy because of the lengthy ingredients list. Putting it together is almost as easy as making a big bowl of steaming ramen noodles with the little foil package. You know, the food most people who've been camping or to college have eaten more of than they care to admit.

2 TBSP BUTTER

2 CUPS TRIMMED AND SLICED SHIITAKE MUSHROOMS (ABOUT 8 OZ/225 G)

KOSHER SALT

5 CUPS/1.2 L UNSALTED CHICKEN OR FISH STOCK (PAGE 27)

1 THUMB-LENGTH PIECE DAIKON OR 4 TO 6 FRENCH BREAKFAST RADISHES

1 THUMB-LENGTH PIECE FRESH GINGER, PEELED

1/2 CUP/6 G ROASTED SHREDDED SEAWEED (KIZAMI NORI)

1 GOLDEN BEET, PEELED AND CUT INTO 1/2-IN/12-MM SLICES

1 TBSP CHILI PASTE (AS NOTED, LOOK FOR LAO LUO ZI BRAND, CHAOTIAN CHILI FROM TAIWAN, BUT THE MORE COMMON HUY FONG FOODS IS JUST FINE)

8 OZ/225 G RAMEN NOODLES

4 EGGS

FOUR 2-OZ/55-G HAKE FILLETS

1 CUP/60 G COARSELY CHOPPED NAPA CABBAGE

8 OZ/240 G PULLED PORK, WARMED

1/4 CUP/25 G THINLY SLICED GREEN ONIONS

1/4 CUP/10 G COARSELY CHOPPED FRESH CILANTRO

In a medium frying pan set over high heat, combine the butter, mushrooms, and $1/4$ tsp of salt. Cook for 8 to 10 minutes or until the edges of the mushrooms begin to brown. Remove them from the hot pan and set aside.

In a large pot, combine 1 tsp of salt, the stock, daikon, ginger, and seaweed. Bring the stock to a boil, cover, reduce the heat, and simmer for 10 minutes. Add the beet and the chili paste, cover, and cook until the beet is tender, 8 to 10 minutes. Taste the stock. It should be rich, spicy, and well salted. Adjust as necessary with additional chili paste or salt. Turn off the heat while you prepare the remaining ingredients.

Bring a large pot of water to a boil. Add the noodles and cook until just tender. Drain and portion out in the bottom of four large, deep bowls. Prepare water to poach the eggs, cooking until the whites are firm but the yolks are still runny.

While the eggs cook, bring the stock back to a simmer over medium heat and add the fish. Cook for 10 to 12 minutes or until you meet no resistance when you insert the tip of a knife into the center of the largest piece. Leave the pot on the heat and use tongs to remove the ginger, beet, and daikon from the stock. Put a beet round in each bowl. Cut the daikon into rounds and put a few in each bowl. Add the cabbage. Place a piece of fish on one side of each bowl. Divide the pork among them, tucking it on one side, opposite the fish. Bring the stock to a boil if it isn't boiling already and pour into the bowls. Place an egg on top of each, garnish with the green onions and the cilantro, and serve. Wow.

FISH NOTE:
Look for red or silver hake. Any white fish will work in this soup, including Pacific or North Atlantic halibut, Pacific or North Atlantic cod. Buy the freshest, most sustainable fish at the market. Avoid: white hake, which is overfished.

PORK-SHRIMP SLIDERS
WITH SPICY-SWEET MAYONNAISE AND RICE NOODLE—CUCUMBER SALAD

SERVES 4

Sliders are everywhere these days. If you're growing weary, this pork and shrimp interpretation will restore your faith in the diminutive sandwich. Depending on your capacity for resisting food you love—we know who we are—you will be eating an embarrassing number of them before the night is done. This is outstanding hot weather food because everything is served either cold or at room temperature. The sweet chili sauce is an ingredient you'll need but may not have on hand. It's inexpensive and lasts practically forever in the refrigerator.

8 OZ/225 G PORK LOIN, PREFERABLY ALL-NATURAL, CUT INTO CHUNKS

8 OZ/225 G SHRIMP, PEELED AND DEVEINED

3½ OZ/100 G BACON (ABOUT 3 PIECES)

5 GREEN ONIONS, WHITE AND TENDER GREEN PARTS

½ CUP/20 G COARSELY CHOPPED FRESH CILANTRO

1 TBSP GRATED FRESH GINGER

1 TBSP CORIANDER SEEDS

1 OR 2 CHILES, SUCH AS SERRANO, STEMMED AND HALVED, WITH SEEDS

½ HEAD GARLIC, CLOVES CRUSHED AND PEELED

2 TBSP FISH SAUCE

½ CUP/120 ML MAYONNAISE

2 TBSP SAMBAL OELEK (HUY FONG BRAND IS MY CHOICE HERE)

2 TBSP SWEET CHILI SAUCE

4 SLIDER BUNS OR 8 PIECES LEVAIN OR OTHER SOURDOUGH BREAD

1 CUP/60 G SHREDDED NAPA CABBAGE

Preheat the oven to 350°F/180°C/gas 4. Combine the pork, shrimp, bacon, green onions, ¼ cup/10 g of the cilantro, the ginger, coriander, chiles, garlic, and fish sauce in the bowl of a food processor with the blade attachment in place. Blend for 2 to 3 minutes, scraping

down the bowl once or twice as needed, until you have a thick, smooth paste. Form the paste into golf-ball-size rounds, lay on a lightly oiled or parchment-covered baking sheet, and then gently flatten. Bake for 8 to 10 minutes or until the patties are just beginning to brown. (They should appear cooked, not pink in the center.) An instant-read thermometer should read 160°F/71°C.

Combine the mayonnaise, sambal, and sweet chili sauce in a small mixing bowl.

Toast the slider buns or bread slices and once they have cooled, smear liberally with the mayonnaise mixture. Add a quarter of the shredded cabbage to the bottom of each bun or half the bread slices, and sprinkle each with some of the remaining 1/4 cup/10 g of cilantro. Place a patty on each and cover with bread.

FISH NOTE:
Buy U.S. farmed or wild-caught shrimp. Alaskan spot prawns and pink shrimp from Oregon are sustainable and very tasty. Avoid: imported shrimp from China and other Asian countries, including India, Malaysia, and Thailand.

— RICE NOODLE—CUCUMBER SALAD —

I eat this noodle salad often in the summer—the salty peanuts, crispy cucumber, slippery noodles, and Thai Basil conspire to make an irresistible dish.

3¾ OZ/105 G BEAN THREAD NOODLES (*MAI FUN*)

2 TBSP PEANUT BUTTER

2 TBSP PEANUT, VEGETABLE, OR LIGHT OLIVE OIL

1 TBSP FISH SAUCE

2 TBSP CHILI-GARLIC PASTE, PREFERABLY HUY FONG FOODS

1 SEEDLESS CUCUMBER, CUT INTO THUMBNAIL-SIZE CHUNKS

1/4 CUP/30 G SALTED ROASTED PEANUTS, CHOPPED

1/4 CUP/10 G COARSELY CHOPPED FRESH MINT (OR SUBSTITUTE 1/2 CUP/20 G CHOPPED FRESH THAI BASIL FOR THE MINT AND THE BASIL)

1/4 CUP/10 G COARSELY CHOPPED FRESH BASIL

Soak the noodles in lukewarm water for 10 minutes or until they are tender. Drain and place in a large mixing bowl. Use clean kitchen scissors to cut the noodles into pieces—just cut away until you have a mix of lengths, most no longer than your finger. In a small bowl mix together the peanut butter, oil, fish sauce, and chili paste. Add the cucumber to the bowl with the noodles and toss the noodles with the dressing. Sprinkle on the peanuts and herbs and serve.

THAI GREEN CURRY
WITH SHRIMP, PEA EGGPLANT, AND SWEET PEPPERS OVER JASMINE RICE WITH SWEET-AND-SOUR SLAW

SERVES 4

This is my Wednesday night curry. Given a decent blender and access to some basic Thai ingredients, it's simple to put together. The bright taste is the best part. You'll find a spicy richness that arrives on your palate without any of the heaviness that can mar other coconut-based curries. If you've never made curry before, it's time to start. You won't look back. Be sure not to shake your coconut milk before you open it—read the recipe to see why, if you don't already know.

3 TBSP THAI FISH SAUCE

1 TBSP SHRIMP PASTE

ONE 6-IN/15-CM PIECE GALANGAL, PEELED AND SLICED

ONE 6-IN/15-CM PIECE FRESH GINGER, PEELED AND SLICED

2 STALKS LEMONGRASS, TENDER WHITE MIDSECTION ONLY, PEELED AND SLICED

3 TO 5 BIRD'S EYE OR OTHER WHOLE HOT CHILES, TOP TRIMMED

1/2 CUP/20 G CHOPPED FRESH CILANTRO STEMS AND ROOTS (RINSE CAREFULLY BEFORE CHOPPING)

ZEST OF 1/2 LEMON, PREFERABLY ORGANIC

ONE 13 1/2-OZ/400-ML CAN UNSWEETENED COCONUT MILK, FULL FAT

2 CUPS/480 ML WATER OR CHICKEN, SHRIMP, OR FISH STOCK (PAGE 27)

8 TO 10 PEA (BABY THAI) EGGPLANTS (ABOUT 8 OZ/225 G), TRIMMED AND CUT INTO BITE-SIZE PIECES

2 KAFFIR LIME LEAVES, LIGHTLY CRUSHED

1 BELL PEPPER, ORANGE OR RED, SEEDED AND CUT INTO THIN STRIPS

1 LB/455 G SHRIMP, PEELED AND DEVEINED

JASMINE RICE (RECIPE FOLLOWS)

1/4 CUP/10 G COARSELY CHOPPED FRESH CILANTRO

1/4 CUP/10 G COARSELY CHOPPED FRESH MINT

In a blender or small food processor, combine the fish sauce, shrimp paste, galangal, ginger, lemongrass, chiles, cilantro stems and roots, and lemon zest. Blend very briefly or until the ingredients are just combined and lightly minced. Scoop the top layer of solidified coconut oil off the top of the can of coconut milk and put it in a Dutch oven or large saucepan set over medium heat. Add the paste from the blender and simmer for 8 to 10 minutes or until the oil begins to separate. Add the remaining coconut water from the can along with the water or stock. Add the eggplants and lime leaves, cover tightly, and simmer gently for 30 minutes over medium-low heat, stirring occasionally. Add the bell pepper and cook for another 5 minutes before adding the shrimp. Large shrimp will take as much as 8 minutes, while rock shrimp will take 2 minutes, at most. Taste and watch. Shrimp turn light orange when cooked. Bite into one—it should pop. (Rubbery, mealy shrimp are poor quality or overcooked—maybe even both!) Taste the curry, adding additional fish sauce or salt, as needed.

Have your rice ready. Serve the curry over the rice in shallow bowls with a good dose of cilantro and mint sprinkled on top.

FISH NOTE:
Buy U.S. farmed or wild-caught shrimp. Alaskan spot prawns and pink shrimp from Oregon are sustainable and very tasty. Avoid: imported shrimp from China and other Asian countries, including India, Malaysia, and Thailand.

— JASMINE RICE —

An elegant, fragrant vehicle for every flavor on your plate.

1½ CUPS/285 G JASMINE RICE, RINSED UNTIL THE WATER RUNS CLEAR AND DRAINED

2¾ CUPS/650 ML WATER

In a medium pot with a tight-fitting lid, combine the rice and the water. Cover and set over medium heat until the water is absorbed and the rice is tender, 10 to 15 minutes.

— SWEET-AND-SOUR SLAW —

Simple, sweet, and a little sour, this slaw goes nicely with the curry. It'll confuse your palate into thinking the curry really isn't all that spicy, causing you to reach for more.

1 LARGE HEAD NAPA CABBAGE (ABOUT 2 LB/910 G), SHREDDED OR FINELY CHOPPED

3 TBSP SWEET CHILI SAUCE

1/4 CUP/60 ML RICE VINEGAR

1 1/2 TSP KOSHER SALT

In a large serving bowl combine the cabbage, sweet chili sauce, rice vinegar, and salt. Mix well, taste, and serve.

KIMCHI OYSTER DOGS
WITH SAMBAL MAYONNAISE,
GREEN BEANS WITH BONITO FLAKES,
AND CRISPY YAMS

SERVES 4

I love a good, all-American hot dog, but I love these "dogs" more. It's all about the spicy, fragrant (tell that to my kids) kimchi with the richness of the mayonnaise on a pillowy bun. I use big, fat Pacific oysters, *Ostrea gigas*, that have been shucked and freshly packed into quart/liter containers. Use fresh, not canned oysters. Shuck your own if you're feeling industrious.

1 CUP/240 ML MUSTARD AÏOLI (PAGE 90) WITHOUT THE MUSTARD OR FULL-FAT STORE-BOUGHT MAYONNAISE

1/4 CUP/60 ML SRIRACHA SAUCE

1 1/2 CUPS/190 G ALL-PURPOSE FLOUR

1 TSP KOSHER SALT

ONE 8-OZ/225-G JAR KIMCHI, HOT OR MILD (MY FAVORITE BRAND IS TOBAGI)

6 TO 8 CUPS/1.4 TO 2 L VEGETABLE OR PEANUT OIL

16 TO 24 OYSTERS, DEPENDING ON THE SIZE (ONE 1-QT/960-ML CONTAINER, PACKED)

8 HOT DOG BUNS, TOASTED (TOP LOADERS ARE MY FAVORITE)

In a small bowl, combine the aïoli and sriracha. Set aside. In a shallow bowl, mix together the flour and salt. Put the kimchi in a bowl to pass at the table.

In a large saucepan or a stockpot, heat the oil over high heat until it reaches 375°F/190°C. You want to have at least 3 in/7.5 cm in the pot. Dredge the oysters in the flour and put them in the oil.

Work in batches so you don't crowd the pot. The oil needs to stay hot, so keep the heat on high unless the oil begins to smoke, in which case you can turn it down. Cook large oysters for 2 minutes or until the coating begins to brown around the edges.

Transfer the cooked oysters to a rack or paper towel-lined plate and keep warm while you finish cooking the remaining oysters.

You can build the first dog for your crowd on a toasted bun with a good dose of the sriracha aïoli, 2 to 3 oysters, and a scattering of kimchi. Or just bring the fixings to the table and let everyone build his or her own dog.

FISH NOTE:
Oysters are a sustainable, farmed species. Think of them the way you think of winegrowing regions: where the oysters come from determines their flavor. It's an ocean version of terroir.

— GREEN BEANS WITH BONITO FLAKES —

I urge you to try this combination, and to employ some really fresh green beans—the kind with a snappy, unbending attitude. The terrific umami flavor is worthwhile on its own, but there's also the joy of watching the bonito flakes melt on the surface of the beans the way the first snowflakes in November vanish as they hit the still-green lawn.

12 OZ/340 G GREEN BEANS, TRIMMED

1 TBSP OLIVE OIL

1/4 TSP KOSHER SALT

SQUEEZE OF FRESH LEMON JUICE

1 HEAPING TBSP BONITO FLAKES

Line your green beans up in bunches on a cutting board and cut them into thin rounds, about 1/4 in/6 mm thick, as if you are cutting up green onions (even smaller than the picture!). In a large frying pan set over medium heat, combine the olive oil, beans, and salt. Cook for about 5 minutes, stirring occasionally, until the beans are still crispy but show flecks of brown on the surface. Transfer to a serving bowl, squeeze just a little lemon over the top, and add the bonito flakes, sprinkling them across the hot beans.

— CRISPY YAMS —

This is an easy to make, not too sweet take on the honest, hardworking tuber.

3 YAMS (ABOUT 2 1/4 LB/1 KG TOTAL), PEELED, CUT INTO 1/2-IN/12-MM SLICES, AND SLICES QUARTERED

2 TBSP LIGHT OLIVE OIL OR VEGETABLE OIL

2 TBSP SOY SAUCE

1/4 CUP/30 G SESAME SEEDS, TOASTED (SEE PAGE 30)

FLAKY OR COARSE SALT

Preheat the oven to 400°F/200°C/gas 6. In a large mixing bowl, toss the yam chunks with the oil and soy sauce until each piece is well coated. Lay the yams out on a baking sheet (line with parchment if you like) and roast for 20 minutes or until the pieces are just showing flecks of black on the edges. Remove from the oven and transfer to a serving bowl. Sprinkle with the sesame seeds and a pinch of flaky or coarse salt.

FRIED SPIDER SANDWICH
WITH AVOCADO AND WAKAME-UDON-SESAME NOODLE SALAD

SERVES 4

This is hangover food of the gods. A pan-Asian rendition of a fried soft-shell crab sandwich—made with a little chili mayo, avocado, and ginger on a soft bun—will fix just about any previous excess.

---

4 SOFT-SHELL CRABS, PREFERABLY CLEANED

8 TO 10 CUPS/2 TO 2.4 L VEGETABLE OIL

½ CUP/120 ML FULL-FAT STORE-BOUGHT MAYONNAISE

1 TBSP CHILI-GARLIC PASTE

3 EGGS

3 CUPS/320 G PANKO CRUMBS, LIGHTLY CRUSHED

KOSHER SALT

4 SOFT SESAME SEED HAMBURGER OR SANDWICH BUNS

1 HASS AVOCADO, PITTED, PEELED, AND SLICED

12 TO 16 SLICES PICKLED GINGER

If you're cleaning the crabs yourself, use scissors to snip off the mouth and eyes of each crab. Next, remove the gills on each side by lifting up the skin on the crab's back. The gills are soft, white, and squishy and will come away easily. Finally, remove the apron (sexual organs) from the back of the crab by snipping them.

In a deep fryer, Dutch oven, or large pot, heat the oil over high heat until it reaches 375°F/190°C. You'll need a depth of at least 3 in/7.5 cm. I prefer to fry two crabs at a time in a smaller pot—mostly to use less oil. Be sure to bring the oil back to 375°F/190°C between batches.

While the oil is heating, mix together the mayonnaise and chili-garlic paste in a small bowl. Set aside.

Beat the eggs together in a small mixing bowl and put the panko in another small bowl next to it. Dip the crab first in the egg and then in the panko, taking care to coat each crab with crumbs as thoroughly as possible. When the oil is hot, add the crabs and cook for 3 to 4 minutes or until the crumbs are a nice toasty brown. Transfer to a paper towel-lined plate, sprinkle with a pinch of salt, and repeat to cook the remaining crabs.

Toast the buns, letting them cool slightly before coating both sides with chili mayonnaise. Layer a quarter of the avocado on the bottom of each bun, and then 3 or 4 slices of ginger. Lay a crab on top and close it up.

FISH NOTE:
Soft-shell crabs should be lively and kicking when you select them. They're pretty simple to clean (a process that kills the crabs), but why not have your fishmonger do it if he's willing? Cleaned or still alive, store the crabs in the refrigerator wrapped loosely in a damp towel.

— WAKAME-UDON-SESAME —
NOODLE SALAD

I adore wakame. It tastes of the sea almost the way oysters do but with a more pronounced vegetal layer. Buckwheat noodles add flavor, heft, and an irresistible slippery texture when mixed with all that fragrant sesame oil. This recipe makes a big bowl of noodles, but they're the most welcome leftovers you'll find in the refrigerator the day after. They won't last long there, believe me.

7 OZ/200 G SOBA NOODLES

1 CUP/30 G DRIED WAKAME SEAWEED

1/4 CUP/30 G SESAME SEEDS, TOASTED
(SEE PAGE 30)

3 TBSP TOASTED SESAME OIL

3 TBSP SOY SAUCE

FLAKY OR COARSE SALT

Bring a large pot of water to a boil. Add the noodles and cook for 2 to 3 minutes or until just tender. Rinse under cold water, drain, and transfer to a large serving bowl. Bring a medium pot of water to boil over high heat. Add the seaweed, turn off the heat, and let stand for 10 minutes. Drain and combine with the noodles along with the sesame seeds, sesame oil, and soy sauce. Use tongs to mix thoroughly. Taste and add a pinch or two of flaky or coarse salt.

CHAPTER 5

SOUTH ASIAN FISH

SOUTH ASIAN FISH

I find many people intimidated by cooking South Asian food. Maybe it's the quantity of spices? The unfamiliarity with the spices? A fear of the purity of this holy dish called "curry"? Whatever the cause, don't fall prey to your fear. The recipes in this chapter are a revelation and ever so much better than you'll find in restaurants, with very few exceptions. Take the plunge.

You'll want to put in an order to Penzeys Spices or another source that sells high quality spices in small quantities. Be sure to have plenty of yellow and brown mustard seeds, turmeric, brown and black cardamom pods, cumin seeds, coriander seeds, cinnamon, and garam masala. In addition, you'll want some chickpea flour, coconut milk, and whole-wheat chapati flour for those Whole-Wheat Rotis (page 181) you're going to become expert at making. Don't forget the lentils!

DRINKS

Make yourself a sweet or salty *lassi*, with mango, yogurt, and ice. If you'd rather drink beer—I would—a pale ale is traditional. I prefer wheat beers, like the very light Hefeweizen. I even pour it over ice and squeeze a lemon on top when my kitchen gets as hot as Mumbai in the dry season.

AT THE TABLE

Indian food is best eaten in one big, celebratory swoop with plenty of dishes on the table all at one time, including relishes and other condiments, plus bread and rice. It's all in the service of the wild mix of flavors and textures that make this food so much fun and such a pleasure to eat with a crowd.

Gather all the prettiest little bowls and ramekins in your kitchen. Fill them up, starting with a dish of serrano chiles, cut into fine rounds; some carrot shredded and macerated in a little vinegar; toasted, unsweetened coconut flakes; chopped roasted cashews; mango chutney—you get the idea. A pot of rice and some roti or store-bought naan for running through the sauce are never out of place.

SWEETS

A rice pudding, with a hint of cardamom, would be in order follow-ing any of the meals in this chapter, and an anise-scented cookie, served with sweet milky tea, would also be welcome and appropriate. Better yet, plan ahead and make a pistachio *kulfi*! Nothing beats this icy, fragrant, creamy concoction.

WHOLE ROASTED BARRAMUNDI
WITH CILANTRO-GINGER SPICE PASTE, ROASTED CAULIFLOWER, AND JASMINE RICE

SERVES 4

This potent spice paste will enliven any fish. Stuffed inside a whole fish, like a fresh barramundi, and then eaten as a sauce with it once cooked, it delivers a bold flavor you won't soon forget. A pot of Jasmine Rice will round out the meal.

1 TSP KOSHER SALT

½ CUP/20 G FRESH CILANTRO LEAVES

3 TBSP GRATED FRESH GINGER

JUICE OF 1 LIME

½ CUP/30 G UNSWEETENED COCONUT FLAKES

2 TBSP COCONUT OR VEGETABLE OIL PLUS MORE FOR RUBBING ON THE FISH SKIN

TWO 1-LB/455-G WHOLE BARRAMUNDI, GUTTED AND SCALED, HEAD LEFT ON

FLAKY OR COARSE SALT

JASMINE RICE (PAGE 155)

Combine the kosher salt, cilantro, ginger, lime juice, coconut, and oil in a blender, food processor, or mortar. Whirl or pound to form a paste. Transfer half of the paste to a small dish, cover, and set it aside (without allowing it to come in contact with the raw fish) until ready to serve. Slash three to four deep slits on each side of the fish. Rub the remaining paste into the slashes and work some into the cavity of the fish. If you have the time, refrigerate the fish for 30 minutes to 1 hour before cooking.

To cook, preheat the oven to 400°F/200°C/gas 6, and set each fish on a long piece of foil on a baking sheet. Crimp the edges up around the fish, 1 or 2 in/2.5 to 5 cm from the fish, to catch the juices. Coat the skin with a little oil and sprinkle with a pinch of flaky or coarse salt before cooking.

Roast the fish for 8 to 10 minutes. Test it while it's in the oven by inserting a knife at the thickest point, where the head meets the body. If you feel little or no resistance, turn on the broiler to high and broil for 3 to 5 minutes to finish the fish. The skin should be toasty brown in spots and the flesh should flake apart. Look for an internal temperature of 135°F/57°C if you're using a thermometer. Serve with the reserved spice paste and Jasmine Rice. (For more on serving whole fish, see page 23.)

FISH NOTE:
Barramundi farmed in the United States and Australia in fully recirculating systems are sustainable. Branzino is a good alternative, as is farmed hybrid striped bass or wild black sea bass.

— ROASTED CAULIFLOWER —

Cauliflower roasted at a high temperature takes on an airy texture and a fine taste that accompanies that blackness. Don't be afraid to leave the cauliflower in the oven—no, you don't want it black all over, but you do want it a little charred.

2 TSP GROUND CUMIN

2 TSP GROUND TURMERIC

2 TBSP OLIVE OIL

½ TSP KOSHER SALT

1 HEAD CAULIFLOWER, BROKEN INTO BITE-SIZE FLORETS

FLAKY OR COARSE SALT

Preheat the oven to 500°F/260°C/gas 10. In a large mixing bowl, mix together the cumin, turmeric, olive oil, and kosher salt. Add the cauliflower and patiently toss until the spice-oil mixture pretty well coats the cauliflower. Spread out the cauliflower on a baking sheet (with or without parchment) and roast for 10 to 12 minutes, or until more than just blackened on the edges—really, the cauliflower should show great streaks of black, and the part touching the baking sheet should be quite dark. Finish with a pinch of flaky or coarse salt.

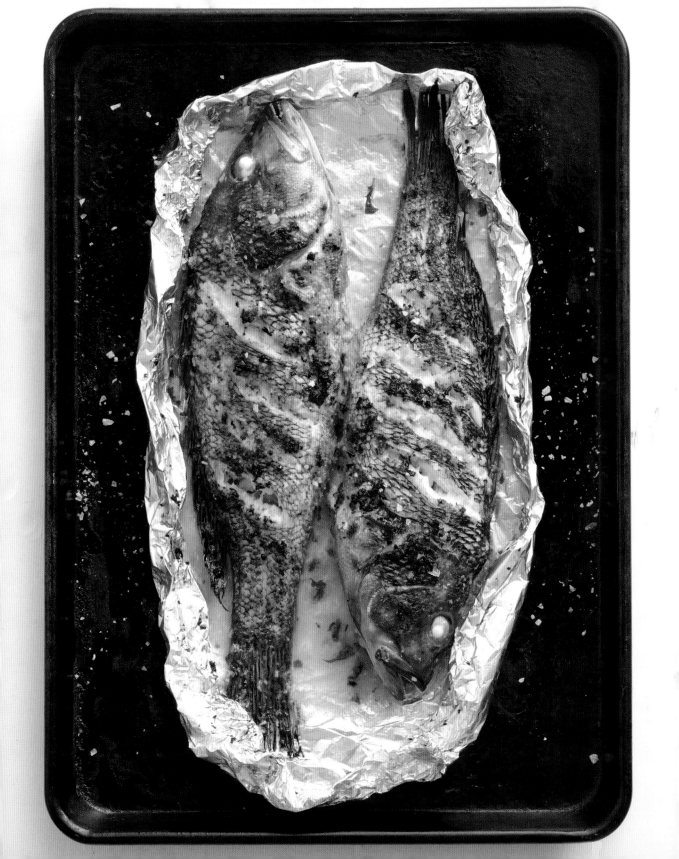

COD WITH CURRIED RED LENTILS,
MUSTARD SEEDS, BASMATI RICE, AND APPLE-CURRANT RELISH

SERVES 4

This is a terrific example of a healthy and unusually tasty braised fish. It's easy to make, and the fish cooks so gently in the liquid that messing it up is all but impossible. Get into the spirit of these flavors by putting out an array of small dishes: bring on a jar of Mixed Pickles (page 183), Whole-Wheat Rotis (page 181), and maybe some Cucumber-Mint Raita (page 193). You'll have an extravagant feast.

2 TBSP OLIVE OIL

1 SWEET ONION, SUCH AS VIDALIA, THINLY SLICED

1 TBSP GARAM MASALA

2 TBSP CURRY POWDER

1 TSP CELERY SEEDS

1 CHILE, SUCH AS SERRANO OR JALAPEÑO, CHOPPED

1 RED BELL PEPPER, SEEDED AND DICED

3 CUPS/480 G RED LENTILS

6 CUPS/1.4 L CHICKEN OR FISH STOCK (PAGE 27) OR WATER

2 TSP KOSHER SALT

12 OZ/340 G COD OR HALIBUT FILLETS, CUT INTO LARGE CHUNKS

FLAKY OR COARSE SALT

1/4 CUP/10 G CHOPPED FRESH CILANTRO

1 LIME, QUARTERED

BASMATI RICE (PAGE 186)

APPLE-CURRANT RELISH (RECIPE FOLLOWS)

In a large frying pan with a lid or a Dutch oven, combine the oil and onion and place over medium-low heat. Cook, stirring frequently, for 15 minutes or until the onion is soft and just beginning to show a little color. Add the garam masala, curry powder, celery seeds, chile, and bell pepper. Stir and cook for another 10 minutes over medium-low heat. Add the lentils and water, stir, and cook for another 20 minutes or until the lentils are tender. Add the kosher salt. You should have a good quantity of flavorful, spicy liquid. If not, add water and bring back to a simmer before adding the fish. Submerge the fish in the liquid as much as possible, cover, and cook for 6 to 8 minutes or until the fish flakes when a fork is inserted into the thickest piece. Sprinkle with salt and cilantro, and serve with the lime, Basmati Rice, and Apple-Currant Relish.

FISH NOTE:
Buy Pacific or North Atlantic cod, Atlantic haddock, or, for a supersustainable choice, U.S. farmed catfish. Avoid: catfish farmed in Asia.

— APPLE-CURRANT RELISH —

This is a lively sweet-and-sour condiment for your curry.

1 GRANNY SMITH OR OTHER TART APPLE, CORED, PEELED, AND CUT INTO DICE-SIZE CHUNKS

2 TBSP FRESH LEMON JUICE

½ CUP/85 G CURRANTS

In a small, pretty bowl toss together the apple chunks with the lemon juice to prevent them from oxidizing. Add the currants and stir to allow the lemon juice to plump the currants.

COD, OKRA, AND CAULIFLOWER CURRY
WITH MUSTARD SEED BASMATI RICE

SERVES 4

The original Tamil word, *kari*, means a spiced sauce. It was the Portuguese who first ran with the word, as *karil*, but it seems that the first curry recipe in English, "To Make a Currey the India Way," comes from Hannah Glasse in 1747. This recipe is also the first evidence that, as Alan Davidson writes in *The Penguin Companion to Food*, "what had been an Indian sauce to go with rice has become an English stew with a little rice in it." Today, there's no escaping the ubiquity of curry as a dish and as a flavor from Boise to Kuala Lumpur. Its meaning and the flavors it denotes are far from fixed. In its best incarnation today, curry remains a stew—layered, fragrant, spicy, complex, and unforgettable. Make this one and see for yourself.

2 TBSP BUTTER

1 SWEET ONION, SUCH AS VIDALIA, HALVED AND THINLY SLICED

1/2 CUP/55 G CASHEWS, GROUND

2 TSP GROUND TURMERIC

1 TBSP YELLOW MUSTARD SEEDS

1 TSP FENUGREEK SEEDS

3 GREEN CARDAMOM PODS

1 BLACK CARDAMOM POD

2 SERRANO CHILES, CUT INTO THIN ROUNDS

2 CURRY LEAVES

2 CUPS/480 ML UNSWEETENED COCONUT MILK

1 TBSP KOSHER SALT

3 CUPS/720 ML CHICKEN, VEGETABLE, OR FISH STOCK (PAGE 27)

1 SMALL HEAD CAULIFLOWER, BROKEN INTO BITE-SIZE FLORETS

10 OKRA PODS, CUT INTO 1/2-INCH/12-MM ROUNDS

ONE 1-LB/455-G COD FILLET OR ANY WHITE, FLAKY, NONOILY FISH

MUSTARD SEED BASMATI RICE (RECIPE FOLLOWS)

1/4 CUP/10 G CHOPPED FRESH CILANTRO

Melt the butter in a large Dutch oven or pot with a lid. Add the onion and sauté over medium-low heat for 30 minutes or until very soft and lightly caramelized. Stir frequently and reduce the heat

if the edges burn. Add the cashews, turmeric, mustard seeds, fenugreek, green and black cardamom, half of the serrano chiles, and
the curry leaves to the pot. Raise the heat to medium and cook for
5 minutes, stirring frequently. Add the fat from the top of the
coconut milk, reserving the coconut water. Stir the fat in with the
spices and cook for another 5 minutes. Add the remaining coconut
water, salt, stock, cauliflower, and okra. Cover and cook over medium
heat for 20 to 25 minutes or until the cauliflower is tender.

Cut the fillet into large chunks—five or six pieces—and nestle
them in the liquid. Cover and cook for 5 minutes. Taste the curry
for salt and spice, line a flat bowl with Mustard Seed Basmati Rice,
and ladle on the curry. Finish by scattering the cilantro over the
top. Put the remaining rounds of serrano chile in a small bowl and
pass them at the table.

FISH NOTE:
Buy Pacific cod, Pacific or North Atlantic haddock, Atlantic cod
from Nova Scotia or Norway, or, for a super sustainable choice, U.S.
farmed catfish. Avoid: catfish farmed in Asia.

— MUSTARD SEED BASMATI RICE —

Buttery rice is one of the (admittedly many) foods that
makes me leave behind the remotest idea of restraint. Add a
few toasted brown mustard seeds and I'm eating right out of the pot
with a serving spoon.

1½ CUPS/285 G BASMATI RICE, RINSED UNTIL THE
WATER RUNS CLEAR AND DRAINED

2¾ CUPS/660 ML WATER

½ TSP KOSHER SALT

4 TBSP/55 G UNSALTED BUTTER

3 TBSP BROWN MUSTARD SEEDS

Put the rice, water, and salt in a saucepan with a tight-fitting lid.
Place over medium heat and cook, covered, for 12 to 15 minutes or
until the water is absorbed and the rice is tender. Let stand. In a
small saucepan melt the butter with the mustard seeds over low
heat until the butter is very hot but not brown. Fluff the rice with
a fork, pour over the butter, and fluff some more until the rice is
coated. Taste for salt. The rice should be delicious all by itself.

GOAN FISH CURRY
WITH SPICY SNAP PEAS AND
WHOLE-WHEAT ROTIS

SERVES 4

Seasoned travelers like to say that Goa is India for beginners—
with its easy, beachy pace, natural beauty, and marked lack of
poverty and squalor. Think of this recipe as curry for beginners:
delicious and memorable but undemanding. Catfish works nicely
here, but any white, flaky fish will do. Don't be afraid of the rotis.
They're simple to make and well worth having on your plate—the
better to sop up that irresistibly spicy yellow sauce.

2 TBSP PEANUT OIL

1 SWEET ONION, SUCH AS VIDALIA, THINLY SLICED

2 TBSP YELLOW MUSTARD SEEDS

1 CINNAMON STICK

1 TSP GROUND TURMERIC

1/2 TSP GARAM MASALA

1 TBSP KOSHER SALT

2 SERRANO, JALAPEÑO, OR DUNDICUT CHILES
(SEE HEAT AND CHILES, PAGE 30)

1 THUMB-LENGTH PIECE FRESH GINGER, PEELED
AND CUT INTO CHUNKS

2 LARGE TOMATOES, CORED

2 CUPS/480 ML WATER

ONE 13 1/2-OZ/400-ML CAN UNSWEETENED
COCONUT MILK, FULL FAT

1 LB/455 G CATFISH FILLETS, OR OTHER WHITE,
FLAKY FISH, CUT INTO 4 OR MORE PORTIONS

BASMATI RICE (PAGE 186)

COCONUT CHUTNEY (SEE PAGE 182)

SPICY SNAP PEAS (RECIPE FOLLOWS)

WHOLE-WHEAT ROTIS (RECIPE FOLLOWS)

Heat a large Dutch oven or a large, deep frying pan over medium heat.
Add the peanut oil, onion, mustard seeds, cinnamon stick, turmeric,
garam masala, and salt. Cook, stirring frequently, for 10 to 12 minutes
or until the onion is very soft and the spices are fragrant.

While the onion cooks, combine the chiles, ginger, tomatoes, and water in a blender. Pulse briefly, just to chop—not purée—the chiles and ginger. It won't take long. Add the liquid to the onion mixture, along with the coconut milk, and stir. Cook, uncovered, over medium-low heat for another 10 to 12 minutes. You can set the curry aside at this point until 10 minutes before you're ready to eat. Reheat the ingredients and add the fish. Cook over medium heat for 8 to 10 minutes or until the fish is flaky. Taste for seasoning and serve over Basmati Rice with the coconut chutney, the Spicy Snap Peas, and the Whole-Wheat Rotis on the side.

FISH NOTE:
Buy U.S. or E.U. farm-raised catfish. Avoid: Asian catfish. Substitute North Atlantic or Pacific cod or North Atlantic or Pacific halibut. Shrimp would also work; just be sure they're not imported from Asia.

— SPICY SNAP PEAS —

You'll be amazed—at least I was—at how a little sass crossing the sugar in the snap peas gives a shine to them and everything else on your plate.

2 TBSP OLIVE OR VEGETABLE OIL, OR BUTTER

1 TSP MEDIUM-HOT CHILE POWDER

1/4 TSP MUSTARD POWDER

1/2 TSP KOSHER SALT

1 LB/455 G SUGAR SNAP PEAS

In a large frying pan set over high heat, combine the oil, chile powder, mustard powder, and salt. Stir to combine the spices with the oil, add the snap peas, and cook for 2 to 3 minutes or until the snap peas show little spots of brown on one or the other side but remain very crispy.

— WHOLE-WHEAT ROTIS —

Try not to think of this as "making bread"—which might make
you turn the page. Think of it as mixing together flour, water,
a little salt, and oil to make one of the most delicious flatbreads
you can imagine. Buy a small bag of whole-wheat chapati flour, a
fine, flavorful flour, and see if you aren't impressed with yourself.
Really. (If you don't have any chapati flour, mix 1 part whole-wheat
flour with 3 parts white flour as a substitute.)

2 CUPS/240 G WHOLE-WHEAT CHAPATI FLOUR,
PLUS MORE FOR DUSTING

1 CUP/240 ML LUKEWARM WATER

½ TSP KOSHER SALT

2 TBSP OLIVE OIL OR MELTED BUTTER, PLUS OIL
FOR COATING THE DOUGH

Combine the flour, water, salt, and olive oil in a mixing bowl or
in the bowl of a stand mixer. Mix together with a wooden spoon or
the paddle attachment until the flour and water adhere. Next,
scatter a clean surface with a little flour and begin kneading
the dough, if working by hand. Alternatively, attach a dough hook
to the mixer and mix at medium speed for 3 minutes (if you don't
have one, just use the paddle attachment). Work until the dough is
smooth and pliable but still sticky. If you're kneading by hand,
try not to use more flour than you need. Either way, get a little
oil on your hands (which helps when you're kneading by hand),
form a ball, and coat the ball with oil before wrapping it in
plastic wrap. Let it rest for at least 30 minutes or for up to
2 hours at room temperature.

Preheat the oven to 175°F/80°C. Place the ball of dough on a clean,
very lightly floured surface and use your palm to flatten it into
a disk. Using a large knife, cut the dough into quarters and cut
each of the quarters in half again to form eight pieces. Roll each
piece into a thin round, about the size of a salad plate. No need to
roll them all at once—roll and cook as you go. Heat a large, well-
seasoned cast-iron pan until it smokes. Place a round of dough in
the pan and cook until it has a few black spots, 2 to 4 minutes.
Flip the roti using your fingers or with the help of tongs. Cook
the other side until it, too, shows dark spots. Set the finished roti
on a plate set in the warming oven and repeat until all the dough
is cooked.

SEARED SCALLOPS
WITH COCONUT CHUTNEY
AND MIXED PICKLES

SERVES 4

This rugged, spicy coconut chutney is unlike any you're likely
to have sampled. When paired with the sweetness of the scallops
and the tart pickles, it makes a meal reminiscent of a trip to
Bangalore. Make a simple pot of Basmati Rice (page 186) or better
yet, Mustard Seed Basmati Rice (page 177) to go with this meal.
A Whole-Wheat Roti (page 181) would also be a welcome addition
to your plate.

COCONUT CHUTNEY

1 CUP/60 G UNSWEETENED COCONUT FLAKES,
TOASTED (SEE PAGE 30)

1/4 CUP/10 G FRESH CILANTRO LEAVES

1/4 CUP/10 G FRESH MINT LEAVES

1 TSP CUMIN SEEDS, TOASTED (SEE PAGE 30)

1/2 TSP KOSHER SALT

JUICE OF 1 LIME

2 TBSP VEGETABLE OIL

16 TO 20 SCALLOPS (DEPENDING ON HOW HUNGRY
YOUR CROWD IS AND HOW BIG THE SCALLOPS ARE)

MIXED PICKLES (RECIPE FOLLOWS)

BASMATI RICE (PAGE 186) OR MUSTARD SEED
BASMATI RICE (PAGE 177)

To make the coconut chutney: combine the coconut, cilantro, mint,
cumin, salt, and lime juice in a blender, food processor, or mortar.
Work to a coarse texture. The herbs should be fairly fine, but the
coconut will remain somewhat chunky. Don't overwork. Transfer to
a small serving bowl and set aside.

Heat the oil in a large frying pan over high heat until the oil
is very hot—if it begins to smoke a little, you'll know you're
there. Add the scallops and cook on one side for about 2 minutes
or until a nice crust forms. Flip the scallops and cook for
another 30 seconds or so on the other side, just long enough to
heat them. Serve them crusty-brown-side up with a layer of the
coconut chutney underneath, a few pickles, and some rice. A feast!

Look for sea scallops, not the smaller bay scallops.
Freshness is everything. The chutney is extremely
versatile—pair it with any fish.

— MIXED PICKLES —

My husband, Dwight, and I are almost always engaged in a mostly
good-humored battle over the amount of space pickles take up in
the refrigerator. He likes all brined things; I like most of them,
too, but maybe it's time for him to get his own all-pickle cooler.
There's no room for anything else. Maybe making my own pickles is
how I get even—or concede the battle? Whatever it is, these are the
ones I reach for. They're a little spicy and taste best after a few
days in the brine. Better than store-bought.

5 OKRA PODS, HALVED LENGTHWISE

10 BITE-SIZE FLORETS CAULIFLOWER

1 CARROT, PEELED AND CUT INTO BATONS

10 GREEN BEANS, TRIMMED

1/2 SEEDLESS OR KIRBY CUCUMBER,
CUT INTO BATONS

4 BITE-SIZE TRIANGLES WATERMELON, INCLUDING
THE FRUIT, WHITE, AND RIND

2 CUPS/480 ML CIDER VINEGAR

1 1/2 CUPS/360 ML WATER

1/2 TSP TURMERIC

1 TSP YELLOW OR BROWN MUSTARD SEEDS

1 TSP WHITE PEPPERCORNS

1/2 TSP CHILE FLAKES

1 TBSP SUGAR

1 TBSP KOSHER SALT

Pack the vegetables and watermelon rind into one or two heat-proof
glass jars with sealable lids. In a medium saucepan set over high
heat, combine the vinegar, water, turmeric, mustard seeds, peppercorns, chile flakes, sugar, and salt. Bring the mixture to a boil
and pour over the vegetables. Top with water as needed. Seal and
refrigerate.

The vegetables are ready to eat as soon as they are cool. They will
get stronger in flavor and more limp in texture over time. You can
keep them for up to 2 weeks.

FRIED OYSTERS,
SPINACH DAL, AND BASMATI RICE
SERVES 4

This is one of those plates that treats all participants equally—
the oysters, while arguably the stars, are really there to play
along with the dal and rice, mixing together and creating combinations of flavor and texture that are memorable and unusual.
If you're not up to making the Whole-Wheat Rotis, buy some naan,
paint on a gloss of melted butter, wrap them tightly in foil,
and heat them up in the oven (200°F/95°C).

2 CUPS/255 G ALL-PURPOSE FLOUR

1 TSP GROUND CORIANDER

1 TSP MEDIUM-HOT CHILE POWDER

1 TSP GROUND TURMERIC

½ TSP CAYENNE PEPPER

KOSHER SALT AND BLACK PEPPER

4 TO 6 CUPS/960 ML TO 1.4 L VEGETABLE OIL

20 TO 24 SHUCKED OYSTERS

SPINACH DAL (RECIPE FOLLOWS)

BASMATI RICE (RECIPE FOLLOWS)

WHOLE-WHEAT ROTIS (PAGE 181)
OR STORE-BOUGHT NAAN

In a shallow bowl, gently whisk together the flour, coriander, chile
powder, turmeric, cayenne, a healthy pinch of salt, and a good grind
of black pepper. In a large, deep frying pan or a deep fryer, heat
the oil over high heat until it reaches 350°F/180°C. (You'll know the
oil is hot enough if it begins to smoke.) There should be enough oil
in the pot so that the oysters will be submerged, even if they are
touching the bottom.

Dredge the oysters in the flour mixture and carefully lower them
into the hot oil in batches. Cook for 2 minutes or until a nice, deep
brown. Roll them over and cook for another 30 seconds before transferring to a paper towel-lined plate. Sprinkle with a pinch of salt,
and serve hot with Spinach Dal, Basmati Rice, and rotis.

FISH NOTE:
Oysters are a sustainable, farmed species. Think of them the way
you think of winegrowing regions: where the oysters come from
determines their flavor.

— SPINACH DAL —

I like to make this with yellow or red lentils, because they cook quickly, and because I'm a sucker for the contrasting colors.

2 TBSP VEGETABLE, PEANUT, OR COCONUT OIL

1 ONION, THINLY SLICED AND THEN COARSELY CHOPPED

¼ CUP/15 G UNSWEETENED COCONUT FLAKES

½ TSP GROUND TURMERIC

1 TSP GROUND CORIANDER

1 TBSP YELLOW OR BROWN MUSTARD SEEDS

1½ CUPS/240 G YELLOW OR RED LENTILS

1½ CUPS/360 ML WATER

1 TSP KOSHER SALT

5 OZ/140 G FRESH BABY SPINACH

In a large frying pan with a lid set over medium heat, combine the oil, onion, coconut, turmeric, coriander, and mustard seeds. Cook for 5 to 8 minutes or until the onion is soft and the mixture is starting to brown very lightly. Transfer the mixture to a small bowl and set aside. Without washing the pan, set it over medium-high heat and add the lentils, water, and salt. Cover and cook for 20 minutes or until the lentils are tender but have not lost their shape. Add the spinach and return the onion mixture to the pan, stirring to mix them in with the lentils. Reduce the heat to low, cover, and cook for 1 to 2 minutes or just long enough to wilt the spinach.

— BASMATI RICE —

Nutty in flavor and a welcome antidote to all those spicy sauces.

1½ CUPS/285 G BASMATI RICE, RINSED UNTIL THE WATER RUNS CLEAR AND DRAINED

1¾ CUPS/420 ML WATER

½ TSP KOSHER SALT

1 TBSP BUTTER

Combine the rice, water, salt, and butter in a pot with a tight-fitting lid. Place over medium heat and cook for 12 to 15 minutes or until the water is absorbed and the rice is tender.

SHRIMP KORMA
WITH CAULIFLOWER AND ZUCCHINI AND CUCUMBER SALAD

SERVES 4

Rich, silky, and bright yellow, this potent combination calls for a
long catalog of spices—but once you have them, it's effortless. Your
reward is a nuanced, complex meal. I can't say enough about the
virtues of taking on a seemingly challenging recipe like this. Do
it once and you won't blink the next time you dream of those flavors.
Better yet, over time it will evolve and become yours entirely.

2 TBSP VEGETABLE OIL OR GHEE (CLARIFIED BUTTER)

1 SWEET ONION, SUCH AS VIDALIA, COARSELY DICED

3 GREEN CARDAMOM PODS

10 WHITE PEPPERCORNS, CRUSHED

1 TBSP CORIANDER SEEDS, CRUSHED

1 TBSP CUMIN SEEDS, CRUSHED

½ TSP FENUGREEK SEEDS, CRUSHED

1 TBSP MINCED FRESH GINGER

1 TSP GROUND TURMERIC

2 TSP KOSHER SALT

1 TSP CELERY SEEDS

1 TBSP FRESH LEMON JUICE OR WHITE VINEGAR

2 SERRANO CHILES, CUT INTO THIN ROUNDS

2 DUNDICUT OR OTHER HOT RED DRIED CHILES

2 MEDIUM TOMATOES, DICED

½ HEAD CAULIFLOWER, BROKEN INTO BITE-SIZE FLORETS

1 ZUCCHINI, CUT INTO BITE-SIZE CHUNKS

1¼ CUPS/300 ML YOGURT

¼ CUP/25 G CHICKPEA FLOUR

1 TO 1½ CUPS/240 TO 360 ML CHICKEN OR FISH STOCK (PAGE 27) OR WATER (DEPENDING ON THE QUANTITY OF LIQUID IN YOUR TOMATOES)

1 LB/455 G SMALL SHRIMP, PEELED AND CLEANED

BASMATI RICE (FACING PAGE)

½ CUP/20 G COARSELY CHOPPED FRESH CILANTRO

In a large Dutch oven or pot set over medium-low heat, combine the
vegetable oil, onion, and cardamom. Cook, stirring frequently, for
10 minutes or until the onion softens. Add the white pepper, coriander, cumin, fenugreek, ginger, turmeric, salt, and celery seeds.

Reduce the heat to low and cook for another 10 minutes, stirring often to prevent the spices from sticking to the bottom of the pot. They should not smoke or burn. Increase the heat to medium and add the lemon juice, serrano, and Dundicut chiles along with the tomatoes. Stir and cook until the oil and liquid separate, 5 to 10 minutes. Add the cauliflower and zucchini, stirring to coat the vegetables with the spice mixture. Turn off the heat.

In a small dish, mix together the yogurt and chickpea flour and add to the pot, stirring as you pour. Mix in the stock and set the pot over medium-low heat. Cook for 10 to 12 minutes or until the cauliflower is tender, stirring often to prevent sticking. Add the shrimp to the pot, submerging them in the hot liquid. Cover and cook for 2 to 3 minutes, depending on the size of the shrimp. Serve over Basmati Rice with the cilantro sprinkled on top.

FISH NOTE:
Wild-caught shrimp and farmed in the United States are the best choices, with wild spot prawns from Alaska and wild pink shrimp from Oregon being the best of the best. How delicious this dish is depends in no small part on the freshness and quality of your shrimp. Buy from a trusted fish shop, and you'll taste the difference in sweetness. Avoid: farm-raised shrimp from Asia, including those from China, India, Thailand, and Malaysia.

— CUCUMBER SALAD —

This is really just a foil for the curry. It's not complicated but it's decidedly refreshing.

1 SEEDLESS CUCUMBER, PEELED IN STRIPS AND CUT INTO 1/2-IN/12-MM CHUNKS

1 TBSP OLIVE OIL

2 TSP CORIANDER SEEDS, TOASTED (SEE PAGE 30) AND LIGHTLY CRUSHED

1 TSP CIDER VINEGAR

1/4 TSP FLAKY OR COARSE SALT

In a small serving bowl, combine the cucumber, olive oil, coriander seeds, vinegar, and salt. Toss and serve.

GRILLED SHRIMP KEBABS
WITH PUNJABI SPICE PAINT AND MIXED SUMMER VEGETABLES

SERVES 4

I concocted the idea of spice "paint" because I was tired of words
like sauce, glaze, mop—you get the idea. The word *paint* seems right
when you use turmeric as much for that lovely ocher yellow color
as for the subtle taste. (There isn't much taste there once it's
ground and dried.) Watch your shrimp turn a lovely coral color as
they grill, all the while toasting the spices to their fragrant
best. It's as if they're trying to keep up. If you crave a starch,
Mustard Seed Basmati Rice (page 177) would be my pick.

4 TBSP/55 G BUTTER OR GHEE (CLARIFIED BUTTER)

1 TSP GROUND TURMERIC

1/2 TSP GROUND CARDAMOM

1/2 TSP CAYENNE PEPPER

1 TSP GROUND CORIANDER

KOSHER SALT

2 TBSP FINELY GRATED FRESH GINGER

2 LB/910 G SHRIMP, PEELED AND DEVEINED

8 CREMINI MUSHROOMS, CAPS ONLY

1 ZUCCHINI OR SUMMER SQUASH, CUT INTO
1 1/2-IN/4-CM CUBES

1 OR 2 BELL PEPPERS OR MILD CHILES,
CUT INTO PIECES

1 TBSP VEGETABLE OR OLIVE OIL

FLAKY OR COARSE SALT

1/4 CUP/10 G COARSELY CHOPPED FRESH CILANTRO

To make the spice paint, combine the butter, turmeric, cardamom,
cayenne, coriander, 1 tsp of kosher salt, and ginger in a small
saucepan and set over low heat. Once the butter melts, leave the pot
on the heat to simmer for 2 to 3 minutes. (If you're using unclari-
fied butter, beware of browning.)

In a large mixing bowl, toss the shrimp with half of the spice paint. Reserve the other half, keeping it barely warm so it doesn't solidify. Thread the shrimp onto skewers without pressing them together. I use metal but if you use wood, be sure to soak them for at least 1 hour.

In a medium mixing bowl, toss the vegetables in the oil and give them a pinch of kosher salt. Work with one vegetable at a time, creating an all-mushroom skewer first, then summer squash, then bell pepper.

Clean and oil the grates of your grill thoroughly. Build a hot fire in a charcoal or wood grill or preheat a gas grill to high. Begin grilling the vegetables before you put the shrimp on. Let them cook until they have a nicely browned exterior and a little char. This may take 8 minutes or it may take 20. It all depends on the size and variety of your vegetables and on how hot your fire is.

When the vegetables are almost done, move them to the side and set the shrimp on the hottest part of the grill. Cook for 3 to 6 minutes, turning once or twice. Because shrimp cook so quickly, I would not close the grill lid. Instead, stand there and baby them as they cook. A quick char over a hot fire is ideal—on and off. When they're cooked, transfer all the skewers to warm plates. Remove the skewers or not, as you prefer. With a pastry brush, dab or brush just a little more of the spice paint on the shrimp—a tad on the vegetables wouldn't hurt, either. Finish by giving everything a pinch of flaky or coarse salt and then scatter the cilantro over it all.

FISH NOTE:
Wild-caught shrimp and farmed from the United States are the best choices, with spot prawns from Alaska and pink shrimp from Oregon being the best of the best. Avoid: farm-raised shrimp from Asia, including those from China, India, Thailand, and Malaysia.

POTATO-CRAB CAKES,
TOMATO-ONION CURRY, BASMATI RICE, AND CUCUMBER-MINT RAITA

SERVES 4

Crab cakes are overrepresented on restaurant menus but underrepresented in home kitchens. I hope this version will have you rethinking the crab cake's place in your kitchen. Here, the sweet, lightly spiced crab in the pancake plays in concert with the potent and utterly delicious Tomato-Onion Curry. Cooling things off in its usual role, a foil for many chiles is the Cucumber-Mint Raita. Don't forget the nutty deliciousness of the Basmati Rice, which soaks up all those flavors in the best possible way.

2 MEDIUM OR 3 SMALL YELLOW OR RED POTATOES, PEELED AND COOKED UNTIL SOFT

12 OZ/340 G LUMP CRABMEAT, PICKED CLEAN

1/4 CUP/25 G CHOPPED GREEN ONIONS

1 TBSP GRATED FRESH GINGER

2 SERRANO OR JALAPEÑO CHILES, CHOPPED

2 TBSP FRESH LEMON JUICE PLUS 1 LEMON, CUT INTO 8 WEDGES

2 EGGS

KOSHER SALT

1/2 TSP TURMERIC

1/2 TSP GARAM MASALA

2 CUPS/255 G ALL-PURPOSE FLOUR

3 TBSP VEGETABLE, PEANUT, OR COCONUT OIL

1/4 CUP/10 G CHOPPED FRESH MINT

TOMATO-ONION CURRY (RECIPE FOLLOWS)

BASMATI RICE (PAGE 186)

CUCUMBER-MINT RAITA (RECIPE FOLLOWS)

Rice the potatoes into a mixing bowl or mash them until smooth. Add the crab, green onions, ginger, chiles, lemon juice, eggs, 1/2 tsp kosher salt, the turmeric, and garam masala. Mix thoroughly. Set out a large plate or tray and form the mixture into golf-ball-size rounds. Roll each one between your palms to form a ball and then flatten to about a 1-in/2.5-cm thickness. You should have about one dozen patties. Put the flour in a shallow dish or bowl and, working in batches, gently dredge the cakes in the flour.

Heat the oil on a griddle or in a large frying pan until it just begins to smoke. Lay some of the cakes in the hot oil and cook for 2 to 3 minutes per side or until each side is toasty brown. Transfer to a paper towel-lined plate, sprinkle generously with kosher salt, and repeat until all the cakes are cooked. Put the crab cakes on a serving plate, tuck the lemon wedges around them, and sprinkle the whole with mint. Pass the Tomato-Onion Curry, Basmati Rice, and Cucumber-Mint Raita at the table.

FISH NOTE:
Buy fresh, never frozen, crab; it will make all the difference. Avoid pasteurized crab if you can help it; it has little sweetness and no ocean flavor.

— TOMATO-ONION CURRY —

This is a surprising accompaniment to the Potato-Crab Cakes. It's simple to make and tastes much better than almost any of the tired Indian food you might happen to eat out.

2 TBSP VEGETABLE, PEANUT, OR COCONUT OIL

1 LARGE RED OR YELLOW ONION, THINLY SLICED

1 CHILE, SUCH AS SERRANO, CHOPPED

1 TSP CUMIN SEEDS

1/4 TSP GROUND TURMERIC

1/4 TSP FENUGREEK SEEDS, GROUND OR WHOLE

1/2 GREEN BELL PEPPER, CHOPPED INTO BITE-SIZE PIECES

3 TOMATOES, COARSELY CHOPPED

1 TSP KOSHER SALT

In a large frying pan set over medium-low heat, combine the oil, onion, chile, cumin, turmeric, and fenugreek. Cook, stirring frequently, for 8 to 10 minutes or until the onion is very soft and the spices are fragrant. Add the bell pepper, tomatoes, and salt and cook for another 8 to 10 minutes or until the mixture begins to stick to the pan. Pile in a bowl and serve.

— CUCUMBER-MINT RAITA —

The hardest-working raita of all—mint and cucumber—can't be beat when it comes to taming the spicy, pungent flavors of the Potato-Crab Cakes and the curry.

3/4 CUP/180 ML PLAIN YOGURT, FULL FAT

1/4 CUP/10 G CHOPPED FRESH MINT

1/2 SEEDLESS CUCUMBER, SHREDDED

In a small, pretty serving bowl combine the yogurt, half the mint, and the cucumber. Stir to thoroughly combine and then top with the remaining mint.

MIDDLE EASTERN AND AFRICAN FISH

MIDDLE EASTERN AND AFRICAN FISH

Romantic, colorful, and exotic are all the clichés that the Middle East and North Africa bring to mind. True to form, this food evokes all of these qualities. It's elegant and sophisticated, with subtle hints of spice and a range of rich ingredients. Have a drink before your meal with a glossy dish of olives, and a plate of Marcona almonds—they're so good when they're really fresh, they hardly seem a product of nature.

You'll want to have access to fresh mint, which makes many appearances here, as well as to high quality saffron (it's expensive!), pearl couscous, sheep's milk feta, and plenty of chickpeas. Chile flakes, millet, dried fruit, and high quality olives will round out the pantry.

DRINKS

If I'm digging into a smoky, sweet hot sauce, I'm reaching for a cold beer. Beyond that, most of the recipes here are quite subtle—well suited to a good bottle of wine from your favorite producer, wherever that might be. For a real treat, consider trying a bottle of Lebanese wine from the legendary Serge Hochar of Chateau Musar. The Prawn-Studded Persian Rice over Wilted Spinach with Olive-Feta Salad (page 213) would be my pick if that's what I was planning to open.

AT THE TABLE

Have a little fun with bright colors—Turkish glasses for water
and wine, colored linens, an extravagant array of candles. Cucumber
rounds floating in a tall pitcher of water make me feel like I'm
somewhere far from home.

Put out squares of pita bread (or your own Whole-Wheat Rotis,
page 181), set out with homemade hummus—easy to make and
mightily superior to store-bought. Drizzle some spicy, fresh
olive oil on top and a sprinkle of sumac and you won't want
for anything else.

SWEETS

Marzipan cake with fresh berries on top is my standard dessert if
I'm throwing a dinner, big or small. I've adapted the recipe from *The
Joy of Cooking*, but there are others. It's really a torte—low, dense,
and flavorful. If you're not up for baking, put out a bunch of
Medjool dates with some dark chocolate and a plate of store-bought
almond cookies.

WHOLE ROASTED BLACK BASS,
FENNEL, AND TOMATOES OVER ARUGULA WITH POMEGRANATE AND MINT

SERVES 4

If I had to pick the healthiest, lowest calorie recipe in *Fish*, this would be it. Depending on how you approach such matters, this may induce you to turn the page or to read hungrily onward with a free and easy conscience. Whatever the state of your conscience—or waistline—try to keep on, even if you lust for fatty, buttery starches and rich sauces. This might be unadulterated fish at its cleanest, most healthful best, but it's also a meal that is super flavorful. If you're lusting for a starch, consider pairing this up with Roasted Eggplant with Pearl Couscous (page 209).

1 LARGE FENNEL BULB, TOUGH OUTER LAYER REMOVED, CUT INTO THIN ROUNDS

2 PT/680 G CHERRY TOMATOES, PREFERABLY SUN GOLD

1 MEDIUM ZUCCHINI OR 2 SMALL, TRIMMED AND CUT INTO 1/4-IN/6-MM ROUNDS

4 TBSP/60 ML OLIVE OIL

KOSHER SALT

1 LEMON, CUT 4 SLICES, WITH THE REMAINDER RESERVED

ONE 2-LB/910-G WHOLE STRIPED BASS, OR 2 SMALLER FISH, GUTTED AND SCALED, HEAD LEFT ON

2 OZ/55 G ARUGULA

1/4 CUP/15 G POMEGRANATE SEEDS

1/4 CUP/10 G CHOPPED FRESH MINT

FLAKY OR COARSE SALT AND BLACK PEPPER

Preheat the oven to 400°F/200°C/gas 6. In a large mixing bowl, combine the fennel, tomatoes, and zucchini. Toss with 2 tbsp of the olive oil and 1/2 tsp of the kosher salt. Line a baking sheet with parchment paper (never mind if you don't have any) and spread the vegetables out in one layer. Lay out the lemon slices over the vegetables in roughly the area where you plan to place the fish.

Rub the fish with 1 tbsp of the remaining olive oil and place the fish over the lemon and vegetables. Sprinkle with 1/4 tsp of kosher salt.

Bake the fish for 15 to 20 minutes, depending on how thick it is. A larger, 2-lb/910-g fish may take up to 25 minutes to cook through. A thermometer should read 135°F/57°C when inserted at the thickest point, where the head meets the body. The flesh should be yielding and flaky when you insert a knife.

To make the plates, toss the arugula with the remaining 1 tbsp of olive oil and a pinch of kosher salt and divide it among the four plates. Portion out the vegetables on top of the greens, setting the lemon to one side. To serve the fish, gently remove the flesh above the vertebrae and then remove the vertebrae, tail, and head to get to the half of the fish still on the plate, and place a slice of lemon on the center of each portion of fish. (If you need more advice, see Serving Whole Fish, page 23.) Any liquid left behind in the pan should be divided among the plates. Sprinkle on the pomegranate seeds, mint, a pinch of flaky or coarse salt, and black pepper. Finish with a squeeze of the reserved lemon, even if it's just a drop or two.

<u>FISH NOTE:</u>
Wild black sea bass or farmed hybrid striped bass would be the best choices, but any whole fish will do. Consider smaller whole fish like porgy (scup), farmed barramundi, branzino, or trout.

PACIFIC HALIBUT
WITH TOMATOES, GARLIC, AND CHICKPEAS, PEARL COUSCOUS, AND RADISH-CLEMENTINE RELISH

SERVES 4

This is one of the simplest yet most sophisticated dishes in *Fish*.
Start to finish, you can have this ready in 30 minutes, and yet,
it will be bright and fresh and unusual in the best possible
way. Do not forego the Radish-Clementine Relish—it's crucial.
Serve with Pearl Couscous.

2 TBSP OLIVE OIL

1 HEAD GARLIC, CLOVES PEELED AND SLICED

3 TOMATOES, COARSELY CHOPPED

1 TSP KOSHER SALT

1 TBSP VINEGAR

1 TSP SUGAR

1/2 TSP CHILE FLAKES

ONE 15-OZ/425-G CAN CHICKPEAS, RINSED

ONE 1-LB/455-G HALIBUT FILLET

PEARL COUSCOUS (RECIPE FOLLOWS)

RADISH-CLEMENTINE RELISH (RECIPE FOLLOWS)

FLAKY OR COARSE SALT

In a large, deep saucepan with a lid or a Dutch oven, combine the
olive oil and garlic and cook over medium-low heat for 2 minutes or
until just fragrant. Add the tomatoes, kosher salt, vinegar, sugar,
chile flakes, and chickpeas and cook for 10 to 12 minutes. At this
point, if you aren't ready to cook the fish, you can turn off the
heat and set the pot aside.

To cook the fish, cut the fillet into pieces about the size of a
dinner roll. Nestle the fish into the liquid, cover, and set over
medium heat for 8 to 10 minutes or until the fish is flaky. To
serve, ladle the fish, chickpeas, and tomato sauce onto one side

of a pasta dish or plate (the sauce will run, of course). Place a portion of the couscous on the opposite side, and flank it with two scoops of the Radish-Clementine Relish. Add a pinch of flaky or coarse salt before serving.

FISH NOTE:
Pacific halibut is sustainable, as is fish from the Baltic Sea (Norway and Russia). Substitute other fish, including Pacific or North Atlantic cod, catfish, or even tilapia. Prawns or shrimp are also an option.

— PEARL COUSCOUS —

Once hard to find on grocery shelves, pearl couscous is easy to come by now and makes a meatier side than regular couscous. It's also sometimes called Israeli couscous.

2½ CUPS/600 ML WATER

2 CUPS/340 G PEARL (ISRAELI) COUSCOUS

1 TBSP VERY GOOD EXTRA-VIRGIN OLIVE OIL

½ TSP KOSHER SALT

½ CUP/55 G KALAMATA OLIVES, COARSELY CHOPPED

¼ CUP/10 G CHOPPED FRESH MINT

In a small saucepan set over high heat, bring the water to a boil. Add the couscous, return the water to a boil, and cook for 5 minutes. Turn off the heat. Let it sit, covered, for 10 minutes. The water should be absorbed and the couscous, tender. Mix in the olive oil, salt, and olives. Sprinkle the mint on top, scattering it across the whole plate, not just on top of the couscous.

— RADISH-CLEMENTINE RELISH —

Another crispy, crunchy, and bright lettuce-free salad.

1 DOZEN FRENCH BREAKFAST RADISHES, TRIMMED AND THINLY SLICED

3 CLEMENTINES, PEELED AND THINLY SLICED TOP TO BOTTOM

¼ TSP KOSHER SALT

2 TBSP VERY GOOD EXTRA-VIRGIN OLIVE OIL

2 TBSP FRESH LEMON JUICE

Toss the radishes, clementines, salt, olive oil, and lemon juice together in a small bowl.

GRILLED MAHI MAHI
OVER COUSCOUS WITH ZA'ATAR, LEMON, AND ASPARAGUS, WITH BLACKENED PEPPERS

SERVES 4

Mahi mahi is an off-white large-flaked fish with a fine, subtle flavor. It cooks easily on the grill, crusted with kosher salt. Never mind if the skin sticks a bit; you won't be eating that anyway. It's just there to protect the flesh, keeping the moisture in. Once you take your fillet off the grill, lay it on a platter over the couscous and then scatter it with the freshly chopped mint.

3 TBSP KOSHER SALT

ONE 1½-LB/680-G MAHI MAHI FILLET, WITH SKIN ON

COUSCOUS WITH ZA'ATAR, LEMON, AND ASPARAGUS (RECIPE FOLLOWS)

BLACKENED PEPPERS (RECIPE FOLLOWS)

1 TBSP VERY GOOD EXTRA-VIRGIN OLIVE OIL

FLAKY OR COARSE SALT

¼ CUP/10 G CHOPPED FRESH MINT

Clean and oil the grates of your grill thoroughly. Build a medium-hot fire in a charcoal or wood grill or preheat a gas grill to medium-high. Press the kosher salt onto the skin side of the fish to coat. Lay the fish on the grill, salt-side down, and cook for 8 to 12 minutes, depending on the thickness of the fish fillet and on how intense your fire is. When the fish begins to feel firm when you poke it with your finger, turn it to cook on the other side just briefly, 3 to 5 minutes.

I love the way this fish looks on a bed of the couscous with herbs on top. Spread out the Couscous with Za'atar, Lemon, and Asparagus on a long platter, and using your largest spatula or a couple of spatulas together, place the fish on top. Tuck the pieces of Blackened Peppers around for color and effect. Finish by drizzling the fish with the olive oil and then sprinkling it with a good pinch of flaky or coarse salt and the chopped mint.

FISH NOTE:
Get troll- or pole-caught wild mahi mahi from the U.S. Atlantic. Avoid imported mahi mahi that is caught by longline. Other market names: dorado, dolphinfish. If you can't find any mahi mahi, try grilling yellowfin tuna, branzino, or trout.

— COUSCOUS WITH ZA'ATAR, — LEMON, AND ASPARAGUS

Fresh mint, almonds, lemon, and couscous—it's hard to go wrong. If it's midsummer, forget about the asparagus and instead use up some of that zucchini. Don't worry if you can't find za'atar. It's not a very specific blend in any case. Just substitute equal quantities of fresh oregano and toasted sesame seeds.

1½ CUPS/360 ML WATER

1 CUP/170 G COUSCOUS

2 BUNCHES (ABOUT 24) ASPARAGUS

5 TBSP/75 ML OLIVE OIL

1 TBSP COLD WATER

1¼ TSP KOSHER SALT

2 TBSP FRESH LEMON JUICE

2 TBSP FINELY CHOPPED FRESH MINT

2 TBSP ZA'ATAR

⅓ CUP/40 G SLIVERED ALMONDS, TOASTED (SEE PAGE 30)

VERY GOOD EXTRA-VIRGIN OLIVE OIL FOR FINISHING

FLAKY OR COARSE SALT

Bring the water to a boil in a medium saucepan with a tight-fitting lid. Add the couscous, cover, remove from the heat, and allow to sit for 5 minutes.

To cook the asparagus, first trim it by holding the ends of each spear and bending it until it snaps, reserving only the top half and discarding the tougher bottom half. You'll want to cut them into delicate pieces no larger than the top of your pinkie above the joint. This may involve cutting some in half lengthwise and then cutting them crosswise into pieces. Put 1 tbsp of the olive oil and 1 tbsp of cold water in the bottom of a large sauté pan and place it over medium-high heat. Put the asparagus in the hot pan and cook, stirring frequently, for 2 to 3 minutes. Add 1/4 tsp of the kosher salt and set the asparagus aside.

In a large mixing bowl, combine the remaining 1/4 cup/60 ml of olive oil, the lemon juice, and the remaining 1 tsp of kosher salt. Add the couscous, using a fork to fluff it as you transfer it to the bowl. Add the mint, za'atar, almonds, and asparagus. Toss to mix and spread out on your platter before drizzling on a little extra-virgin olive oil and a pinch of flaky or coarse salt.

— BLACKENED PEPPERS —

Any mixture of peppers and mildly spicy chiles will work here. An orange or red bell pepper mixed with an Anaheim, Fresno, pasilla, or padrón chile, or a banana, cherry, or shishito pepper would be terrific. That way, you get the sweetness of the bell and a little surprise of heat with the other varieties. How hot they are will depend on growing conditions and the luck of the draw.

6 TO 8 PEPPERS AND CHILES, MIXED VARIETIES, SEEDED AND HALVED OR QUARTERED, DEPENDING ON SIZE

2 TBSP OLIVE OIL

1/2 TSP KOSHER SALT

FLAKY OR COARSE SALT

Preheat the oven to 500°F/260°C/gas 10. Toss the cut peppers and chiles in a large mixing bowl with the olive oil and kosher salt. Spread them out on a baking sheet and roast for 10 to 12 minutes or until the edges and spots on the skin begin to blacken. Sprinkle with a pinch of flaky or coarse salt before serving.

If you prefer, grill the peppers right away along with the fish. They'll take 15 to 20 minutes, depending on your grill, so put them on well before you cook the fish.

ARCTIC CHAR
WITH CHARMOULA,
ROASTED EGGPLANT WITH PEARL
COUSCOUS, AND MINT

SERVES 4

Charmoula, like salsa verde and harissa, is versatile but never dull. The alchemy relies on lemon juice, garlic, chile flakes, olive oil, and herbs. It pairs magically with any protein, delivering acidity, spice, and freshness. Tunisia, Morocco, Algeria—each can lay claim to the sauce. It's magnificent with everything on your plate.

CHARMOULA

1/4 CUP/60 ML FRESH LEMON JUICE

GRATED ZEST OF 1 LEMON

1 TSP CHILE FLAKES

1 TSP CORIANDER SEEDS, CRUSHED

1 TSP CUMIN SEEDS, CRUSHED

1 SHALLOT, MINCED

1/2 CUP/20 G FINELY CHOPPED FRESH PARSLEY

1/2 CUP/20 G FINELY CHOPPED FRESH CILANTRO

2 GARLIC CLOVES, MINCED

1/4 CUP/60 ML VERY GOOD EXTRA-VIRGIN OLIVE OIL

1/4 TSP KOSHER SALT

FOUR 4- TO 6-OZ/115- TO 170-G ARCTIC CHAR FILLETS

1 TBSP OLIVE OIL

1/2 TSP KOSHER SALT

ROASTED EGGPLANT WITH PEARL COUSCOUS (RECIPE FOLLOWS)

1/4 CUP/10 G CHOPPED FRESH MINT

To make the charmoula, in a small serving bowl, mix together the lemon juice and zest, chile flakes, coriander seeds, cumin seeds, shallot, parsley, cilantro, garlic, extra-virgin olive oil, and 1/4 tsp salt. Stir and set aside.

Preheat the broiler to high, positioning a rack as close to the heat source as possible. Line a baking sheet or large, ovenproof frying pan with foil, crimping the edges up all around to catch any liquid that will be released by the fish. Brush the Arctic char with the olive oil, sprinkle with the 1/2 tsp salt, and set it on the foil.

Cook the fish, without turning, for 6 to 12 minutes—possibly more or less, depending on the thickness of the fish and the intensity of your broiler. Check the fish by inserting a knife into the thickest part. The fish should flake apart without resistance. A thermometer inserted into the thickest part of the fish should read 135°F/57°C.

Spoon a little charmoula in the center of each plate, place the fish on top to one side, and a portion of the Roasted Eggplant with Pearl Couscous on the other. Sprinkle with mint and serve.

<hr>

FISH NOTE:
Wild Alaskan salmon or coho salmon are the closest alternatives to Arctic char. Truth is, the charmoula will pair up with any fish.

— ROASTED EGGPLANT WITH — PEARL COUSCOUS

Eggplant is one of the most difficult vegetables to cook. It must be cooked thoroughly or it will have that acrid searing effect on the roof of the mouth that's far from pleasant. This recipe will insure that your eggplant is cooked, but you won't need to soak it in oil as you do when frying it.

1 LARGE EGGPLANT (ABOUT 2 LB/910 G), CUT INTO 1-IN/ 2.5-CM CUBES

2 TBSP OLIVE OIL

3/4 TSP KOSHER SALT

2 1/2 CUPS/600 ML WATER

2 CUPS/340 G PEARL (ISRAELI) COUSCOUS

1 TBSP VERY GOOD EXTRA-VIRGIN OLIVE OIL

Preheat the oven to 400°F/200°C/gas 6. In a mixing bowl, toss the eggplant with the olive oil and 1/4 tsp of the kosher salt. Lay the eggplant on a baking sheet (line with parchment if you like) and roast for 20 to 30 minutes or until the eggplant is soft and shows flecks of brown and black on the edges.

In a small saucepan set over high heat, bring the water to a boil. Add the couscous, return the water to a boil, cover and simmer for 5 minutes. Turn off the heat and let it sit, covered, for 10 minutes. The water should be absorbed and the couscous, tender.

Transfer the couscous to a large mixing bowl and toss with the extra-virgin olive oil and remaining 1/2 tsp of the kosher salt. Add the roasted eggplant and toss again.

GRILLED TUNA SKEWERS
WITH SMOKY SWEET HOT SAUCE AND FATTOUSH

SERVES 4

What I like best about this meal is the intense flavor of homemade hot sauce with the meaty sweetness of rare tuna. On the plate with the Fattoush, a classic Lebanese pita bread salad, this is a tantalizing meal that yields grand results in return for a minimum of time and effort.

1½ LB/680 G YELLOWFIN TUNA FILLETS OR STEAKS, CUT INTO 1½-IN/4-CM CHUNKS

½ TSP KOSHER SALT

1 TBSP VEGETABLE OR PEANUT OIL

In a mixing bowl, toss the tuna with the kosher salt and oil. Thread the fish onto either metal skewers or wood skewers that have been soaked in water for at least 1 hour.

Clean and oil the grates of your grill thoroughly. Build a hot fire in a charcoal or wood grill or preheat a gas grill to high. (If you prefer to use the broiler, follow the instructions on page 23.)

Set the tuna skewers on the hottest part of grill. Cook for 2 to 6 minutes, turning once. Because tuna cooks so quickly, I would not close the grill lid. Instead, stand there and baby the fish as it cooks. A little quick char is ideal—on and off. Overcooked tuna is gray and dry. When they're cooked, transfer all the skewers to warm plates. Remove the skewers or not, as you prefer.

FISH NOTE:
Look for troll- or pole-caught yellowfin tuna from U.S. or E.U. waters. If you can't find tuna, you'll need to substitute another meaty fish that will stay on the skewers, such as mahi mahi.

— SMOKY SWEET HOT SAUCE —

This is a take on one of my favorite and most-used recipes in *Poulet*, my second cookbook. There it is called Raw Hot Sauce. It's a simple sauce—really almost a relish—you make using fresh chiles, a little salt, and the juice of a lime. Here, I've added a sweet pepper and given the sauce a smoky taste by blackening the chiles. See if it doesn't change your mind forever about which hot sauce you put on *everything*. If you don't like your hot sauce incendiary, omit the habanero and add another serrano.

If you're out of time or feeling lazy, skip the blackening and just make the sauce with raw peppers and chiles. It's terrific that way, too.

½ RED OR ORANGE BELL PEPPER, SEEDED AND CORED

2 SERRANO CHILES, STEMMED

1 HABANERO CHILE, STEMMED

JUICE OF 1 LIME

1 TSP KOSHER SALT

To blacken the sweet pepper and chiles, first preheat the oven to 500°F/260°C/gas 10. Put the pepper and chiles on a baking sheet and roast in the oven for 12 to 14 minutes until well flecked with black. (A convection oven won't take as long.) Alternatively, put them directly on the hot grill or in a grill basket, and blacken them.

Once the chiles and pepper are cool enough to handle, spread them out on a cutting surface and mince. Put them in a small jar—don't leave the black bits behind on the cutting board! Add the lime juice and salt, cover, and give the jar a shake. Spicy, smoky-good. It'll last 1 week to 10 days in the refrigerator, losing its heat before it actually spoils.

— FATTOUSH —

Middle Eastern bread salad to eat daily. This is a brilliant combination of flavors and textures. Don't shy away from the long list
of ingredients—it all goes in one big bowl.

5 WHOLE-WHEAT PITA BREADS

2 TBSP BUTTER, MELTED

KOSHER SALT

1 FENNEL BULB, TOUGH OUTER LAYER REMOVED, CUT
INTO BITE-SIZE PIECES

12 FRENCH BREAKFAST RADISHES, TRIMMED AND
THINLY SLICED

1 BLOOD ORANGE, PEELED AND CUT INTO BITE-SIZE
CHUNKS (SUBSTITUTE A NAVEL OR TANGELO)

3 1/2 OZ/100 G FETA CHEESE, CRUMBLED INTO
COARSE CHUNKS

1 CUCUMBER, PEELED AND CUT INTO BITE-SIZE
PIECES

1 ARTICHOKE HEART, STEAMED AND CUT INTO
BITE-SIZE PIECES

1/4 CUP/10 G COARSELY CHOPPED FRESH MINT

2 TBSP GROUND SUMAC

5 OZ/140 G ARUGULA

3 TBSP OLIVE OIL

2 TBSP FRESH LEMON JUICE

3 TBSP SESAME SEEDS, TOASTED (SEE PAGE 30)

Brush the pita bread with the butter, using it all. Sprinkle with
a pinch of salt and place on the grill over medium to hot coals
before you grill your tuna. When the pita breads have dried out
and show a few black spots and a stripe here and there, take them
off the fire and break them into bite-size pieces in a large salad
bowl. Add the fennel, radishes, orange, feta, cucumber, artichoke
heart, mint, sumac, and arugula. Do not toss. Just before serving, add
the olive oil, lemon juice, and 1/2 tsp of salt, toss, and sprinkle
with the sesame seeds.

PRAWN-STUDDED PERSIAN RICE
OVER WILTED SPINACH WITH
OLIVE-FETA SALAD

SERVES 4

My friend Jonny Miles, a first-rate cook who always has some adventurous meal bubbling on his stove top, served me Persian rice the first time. In that case there were no shrimp, but there was a lovely, buttery, crusty bottom that I just couldn't get enough of. This crispy layer from the bottom of the pot has a name in Persian, *tah dig*. I've made this decadent rice into a one-plate meal that I find calling out to me—buttery, crispy, fruity, nutty—whenever I find my soul in need of pampering—and butter.

2 CUPS/380 G LONG-GRAIN RICE

KOSHER SALT

6 TBSP/85 G BUTTER

12 THREADS SAFFRON (MAKE SURE YOUR SAFFRON IS FRESH—IT'LL BE FLAVORLESS IF IT'S BEEN LANGUISHING IN YOUR SPICE CABINET)

1 SHALLOT, FINELY CHOPPED

1/2 ORANGE OR RED BELL PEPPER, SEEDED AND DICED

1 TSP CUMIN SEEDS

1/4 TSP GROUND CINNAMON

1 LB/455 G SHRIMP (CHOOSE THE FRESHEST AND BEST, REGARDLESS OF SIZE)

FLAKY OR COARSE SALT AND BLACK PEPPER

1/3 CUP/45 G RAISINS, GOLDEN, BLACK, OR A MIXTURE OF THE TWO

12 DRIED APRICOT HALVES, CHOPPED

ZEST OF 1 LEMON, GRATED

1 TBSP OLIVE OIL

5 OZ/140 G FRESH BABY SPINACH

1/4 CUP/10 G CHOPPED FRESH PARSLEY

3/4 CUP/100 G SLIVERED ALMONDS, TOASTED (SEE PAGE 30)

⇨

Bring a large pot of water to a boil over high heat. Add the rice and 1 tbsp kosher salt and boil for 7 minutes. Drain and set aside. Melt 3 tbsp of the butter and combine it with the saffron in a small dish. Set aside. In a large, heavy saucepan (cast-iron is ideal), melt 2 tbsp of the butter over medium heat. Add the shallot, bell pepper, cumin, and cinnamon. Cook for 3 to 5 minutes or until the bell pepper is slightly softened. Add the shrimp and cook for 1 to 2 minutes or until they just begin to color orange. Season with flaky or coarse salt and pepper and transfer the shrimp-bell pepper mixture to a small bowl and set aside.

In the same frying pan melt the remaining 1 tbsp of butter over very low heat. Turn off the heat and add half of the parboiled rice, patting it down into an even layer with a wooden spoon or rubber spatula. Spread out the raisins and apricots over the rice in an even layer. On top of that, spread the shrimp-bell pepper mixture. Scatter the lemon zest before adding the remaining rice in another smooth, even layer. Pour the saffron butter as evenly as possible over the top of the rice. Return the pan to very low heat and cover. Cook for 25 to 30 minutes and turn off the heat. Be sure the rice isn't burning—it should be browning but not actually burning. Once cooked, let the rice rest for 15 minutes before serving.

When ready to serve, heat the oil in a large frying pan. Add the spinach, toss, and cook for 1 minute before turning off the heat. Add a pinch of kosher salt and set aside.

Place a portion of the wilted spinach on each plate. Use a spatula to portion out the rice, including some of the bottom crust, on the plate. Scatter on the parsley, almonds, and a pinch of flaky or coarse salt. (If you're feeling really confident about your crust, you can loosen the rice from the sides of the pan with a knife and then invert the pan onto a plate. It's a gorgeous thing to bring to the table.)

FISH NOTE:
Use either shrimp or prawns. Wild-caught shrimp and farmed from the United States are the best choice, with spot prawns from Alaska and pink shrimp from Oregon being the best of the best. Avoid: farm-raised shrimp from Asia, including those from China, India, Thailand, and Malaysia.

— OLIVE-FETA SALAD —

More of a piquant relish than a salad. Make this with the best
olives you can find—that means you take the pits out yourself—
and French sheep's milk cheese.

1 CUP/115 G KALAMATA OLIVES, PITTED AND HALVED

1/4 CUP/25 G DRY-CURED OLIVES, PITTED
AND HALVED

3 1/2 OZ/100 G SHEEP'S MILK FETA CHEESE,
CRUMBLED

3 GREEN ONIONS, THINLY SLICED

In a medium serving bowl, combine the kalamata and dry-cured
olives together with the feta and green onions. Toss and then
let sit for 15 to 20 minutes or for up to 1 hour on the counter
before serving.

SENEGALESE SHRIMP STEW
OVER MILLET
WITH COLLARD GREENS

SERVES 4

This is just the sort of recipe that I take pride in dreaming up—a pot of succulent shrimp with plenty of zing that'll be on your plate in under a hour. In this case, I had fallen for the lovely fresh shrimp at the fish market but hadn't done any other shopping. With coconut milk in the cupboard, a few chiles, and a lime that was likely to end up in someone's gin and tonic if I didn't get to it first, I threw it all together. Don't underestimate this bright, simple, one-plate meal, which recalls Senegalese cuisine with its millet, shrimp, lime, cashews, and spice.

2 TBSP OLIVE OR COCONUT OIL

1 ONION, CHOPPED

1 TBSP SHREDDED FRESH GINGER

1 SERRANO OR JALAPEÑO CHILE, CHOPPED, WITH SEEDS

3 GARLIC CLOVES, CHOPPED

1 CUP/115 G SALTED ROASTED CASHEWS

ONE 13½-OZ/400-ML CAN UNSWEETENED COCONUT MILK, FULL FAT

2 CUPS/480 ML CHICKEN OR FISH STOCK (PAGE 27) OR WATER

1 TSP KOSHER SALT

JUICE OF 1 LIME

1 LB/455 G SHRIMP, SHELLED AND DEVEINED

MILLET (RECIPE FOLLOWS)

¼ CUP/10 G CHOPPED FRESH CILANTRO

In a Dutch oven or large pot set over medium heat, combine the oil and onion. Cook the onion for 5 to 8 minutes, stirring frequently, until soft. Add the ginger, chile, and garlic. Cook for 3 to 5 minutes or until fragrant, stirring often. Chop one-third of the cashews as finely as you can and add them to the pot along with the coconut milk, stock, and salt. Cover and simmer for 15 minutes then add lime juice. Coarsely chop the remaining cashews and set aside. Add the shrimp and cook until just pink—about 3 minutes. Serve over the Millet with cilantro and chopped cashews scattered on top.

FISH NOTE:
Wild-caught shrimp and farmed from the United States are the best choices, with spot prawns from Alaska and pink shrimp from Oregon being the best of the best. Avoid: farm-raised shrimp from Asia, including those from China, India, Thailand, and Malaysia.

— MILLET —

Millet is a staple in Africa, where a great deal of it is grown. It deserves a bigger place in the kitchen repertoire on this continent. Toasty, nutty, and easy to make—consider it a welcome departure from rice and potatoes.

1 CUP/200 G MILLET, TOASTED (SEE PAGE 30)   ½ TSP KOSHER SALT

1 TBSP OLIVE OR COCONUT OIL

Cook the millet as you would pasta in a large pot of water. Boil for 25 minutes, drain, and toss with the oil and salt. The millet should be perfectly salted on its own—adjust accordingly.

— COLLARD GREENS —

My husband, Dwight, who was born in West Virginia, fondly remembers his grandmother Mary's collards—pressure-cooked to dull green submission, with plenty of bacon for a smoky, fatty edge. We always disagree about how to cook greens of any kind. I prefer mine, even my collards, to remain recognizable as the plant they once were. Here's my recipe for distinctively ungrandmotherly collards. Cook them longer if you must.

2 TBSP BUTTER OR COCONUT OIL

1 BUNCH COLLARD GREENS, RINSED (BUT NOT DRIED), AND CUT INTO RIBBONS

½ TSP KOSHER SALT

1 TBSP WATER

FLAKY OR COARSE SALT

The collards should still be wet from rinsing. In a large frying pan with a lid set over medium-low heat, melt the butter. Add the collards along with the kosher salt and water. Cover tightly and cook for 20 to 25 minutes, stirring once or twice to be sure the pan has not dried out, which would scorch the leaves. Add a little more water if the pan is dry and turn down the heat. When properly cooked, the collards should be soft but not shapeless, with plenty of vibrant green color left in them. Add a little pinch of flaky or coarse salt and serve.

BRAISED SQUID
WITH CHERRY TOMATOES, CHICKPEAS, EGGPLANT, AND OREGANO WITH KALE SALAD

SERVES 4

Squid can be tricky to cook. It either needs to be cooked quickly at high temperature, as you do when you fry it, or slow-cooked to tenderize all that connective tissue. This recipe involves a simple two-stage process. First, you slow-cook the squid with some eggplant and other tasty morsels in the oven. You can walk away and forget about it while it's undergoing a delicious transformation. Second, you remove the pot from the oven, add some fresh herbs, tomatoes, and chickpeas and finish it up on the top of the stove. I'd serve it over Roasted Eggplant with Pearl Couscous, leaving out the eggplant (page 209).

¼ CUP/60 ML OLIVE OIL

1 SWEET ONION, SUCH AS VIDALIA, THINLY SLICED

½ HEAD GARLIC, CLOVES PEELED AND LIGHTLY CRUSHED

1 LB/455 G SQUID, CLEANED

1 MEDIUM EGGPLANT (ABOUT 1 LB/455 G), DICED

3 TINNED ANCHOVY FILLETS, CHOPPED

2 CUPS/480 ML DRY WHITE WINE

2 CUPS/480 ML FISH STOCK (PAGE 27) OR WATER

2½ CUPS/455 G DRIED CHICKPEAS

2 CUPS/160 G CHERRY TOMATOES, HALVED

12 KALAMATA OLIVES, PITTED AND COARSELY CHOPPED

¼ CUP/60 ML FRESH LEMON JUICE

½ TSP KOSHER SALT

1 TSP CHILE FLAKES

4 LARGE SPRIGS FRESH THYME

FLAKY OR COARSE SALT

¼ CUP/10 G COARSELY CHOPPED FRESH OREGANO

¼ CUP/10 G COARSELY CHOPPED FRESH PARSLEY

Preheat the oven to 400°F/200°C/gas 6. In a Dutch oven or large ovenproof saucepan set over medium heat, combine the olive oil and onion. Cook for 8 to 10 minutes, stirring frequently, until the onion is soft. Add the garlic and sauté for another minute or two, until just fragrant. Cut the body of the squid from the head down into rounds, stopping at the tentacles, which should be left attached to the body unless they are very large. Add the squid to the pot along with the eggplant, anchovies, white wine, and stock. Cook, tightly covered, in the oven for 40 to 50 minutes or until the squid is tender.

Remove the pot from the oven and add the chickpeas, tomatoes, olives, lemon juice, kosher salt, chile flakes, and 2 of the sprigs of thyme. Set over low heat and cook, covered, for 10 minutes. Taste for salt and sprinkle with flaky or coarse salt. Stem the remaining two sprigs of thyme. Serve in bowls, sprinkled generously with thyme leaves, oregano, and parsley.

FISH NOTE:
Longfin squid from the U.S. Atlantic are sustainable and abundant. If you prefer, you could make this recipe with shrimp. Simply follow the instructions as written, but add the shrimp at the last minute, cooking them for 3 to 8 minutes, depending on how big they are.

— KALE SALAD —

I've never been a fan of kale as a salad green, with the exception of the tiny little leaves that find their way into the most perfect spring mixes. I changed my mind about the virtues of mature kale as a salad green when I discovered that an hour of macerating in lemon juice softens it into something between a gently cooked, wilted green and a fresh, crispy leaf.

4 TO 5 CUPS/100 TO 125 G FINE RIBBONS OF DERIBBED KALE

JUICE OF 1 LEMON

¼ TSP KOSHER SALT

3 TBSP OLIVE OIL

FLAKY OR COARSE SALT

In a serving bowl, combine the kale with the lemon juice and kosher salt. Toss to coat the leaves, cover, and refrigerate for at least 30 minutes or up to 2 hours. When you're ready to eat, add the olive oil and a pinch of flaky or coarse salt, toss, and serve.

INDEX

ACKNOWLEDGMENTS

This book is for my husband, Dwight Garner. He eats fish with more ardor than anyone I know; he's the one I cook for and, aside from myself, aspire to please. Thanks for twenty years of love, appetite, and cleaning the kitchen. A word of thanks to my children, Penn and Harriet. I'll write a cake book someday soon, I promise.

Two more men have my gratitude for making *Fish* a reality. David McCormick, my unfailingly loyal, insightful agent, shepherded this book into the right hands on my behalf. Bill LeBlond, visionary acquisitions editor at Chronicle Books, had the imagination to see *Fish* as a natural sequel to *Poulet*.

Hearty thanks to Sarah Billingsley, my smart, responsive editor at Chronicle Books. To Deborah Kops, the most capable copy editor, thank you. At Chronicle Books, I'd also like to thank designer Sara Schneider who did such an inspired job making *Fish* into a beautiful book. To Antonis Achilleos, your photographs are a gorgeous gift. Looking at them, I can practically smell the ocean.

The Monterey Bay Aquarium's Seafood Watch program provides research and advice on choosing sustainable fish, all available online. This resource was indispensable to making *Fish* the book it is. Thank you to Kyle Riley, fish manager at the Shop Rite in Flemington, New Jersey, for the affordable fish and long chats about what it takes to buy and keep fresh fish in a supermarket. I must also thank Mark Drabich and his manly crew at Metropolitan Seafood in Lebanon, New Jersey, for spoiling me with the freshest fish I've ever eaten. I'm indebted to my cousin Scott Kraus, vice president for research at the New England Aquarium. He knows a thing or two about fish and—better yet—knows people who know even more than he does about which ones we should be eating. Thank you, Scott, for reviewing the sections on sustainable seafood choices and for passing my work along to your colleagues at the aquarium, including Matt Thompson and Jason Clermont, analysts for Sustainable Seafood Advisory Services in the Conservation Department. Matt and Jason, many thanks for sharing your expertise. Thanks as well to Heather Tausig, vice president for conservation. Any remaining errors are, of course, my own. Finally, a word of gratitude to Harold McGee for his masterwork *On Food and Cooking*. If I had to keep just one food book and get rid of the rest, his would be the one left on the shelf.